Key Stage 3 Mathematics
Numeracy Strategy Book 1

This book has been *written specifically* to
cover the Numeracy Strategy at levels 4-5.

Each page contains questions covering a topic of the
Numeracy Strategy. Tips have also been included for
some of the more difficult questions.

And there's even the odd ever-so-nearly entertaining bit,
just to help keep you awake.

What CGP is all about

Our sole aim here at CGP is to produce the highest quality
books — carefully written, immaculately presented
and dangerously close to being funny.

Then we work our socks off to get them out to you
— at the cheapest possible prices.

Contents

Contents

Section Five — Shape, Space and Measures

Section Six — Handling Data

Published by Coordination Group Publications Ltd.

Contributors:

Charley Darbishire

Deborah Dobson

Also Starring:

Chris Dennett

Toby Langley

Tessa Moulton

Iain Nash

Andy Park

Claire Thompson

James Paul Wallis

With Thanks to:

Angela Ryder and Gemma Hallam for the proofreading.

ISBN-10: 1 84146 046 X

ISBN-13: 978 1 84146 046 8

Groovy website: www.cgpbooks.co.uk

Printed by Elanders Hindson Ltd, Newcastle upon Tyne.

Place Value and Ordering

Q1 What are the largest and the smallest numbers that can be made with these sets of digits? Write each number out in words.

 a) 4, 7, 9, 1

 b) 4, 7, 9, 1, and a decimal point

 c) 3, 0, 4, 9

 d) 3, 0, 4, 9, and a decimal point

 e) 1, 2, 3, 7, 8

 f) 1, 2, 3, 7, 9

Q2 What value does the digit 8 represent in each of these numbers?

 a)   548.9

 b)   784.2

 c)   76.8

 d)   4.081

 e)   86560

 f)   9.548

 g)   7801

 h)   823456

 i)   18450

Q3 How much change would Fred get from his £10 birthday money if he bought:

 a)   A magazine costing £3.10?

 b)   A glue gun costing £7.98?

 c)   Shin pads costing £8.46?

 d)   A cap costing £7.63?

> I should never have let Fred get that glue...

Q4 Write out the next four numbers in each of these four sequences.

 a)   1.2   1.3   1.4   1.5   ....

 b)   6.14   6.15   6.16   6.17   ....

 c)   9.4   9.3   9.2   9.1   ....

 d)   0.56   0.55   0.54   0.53   ....

Q5 Work out these sums. Then write down which have the same answer.

 a) $3.4 \times 100 =$

 b) $34 \times 0.1 =$

 c) $2.7 \div 10 =$

 d) $340 \div 100 =$

 e) $0.27 \times 100 =$

 f) $3400 \times 0.1 =$

> *Multiplying* a positive number by 10 or 100 or 1000 etc. makes the number <u>bigger</u>.
>
> *Dividing* a positive number by 10 or 100 or 1000 etc. makes the number <u>smaller</u>.

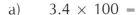

Q6   Fill in the blanks:

 a) $5.2 \times 100 = 5.2 \div ....$

 b) $67 \div 100 = 67 \times ....$

 c) $0.7 \times 100 = 0.7 \div .....$

 d) $8000 \times 0.01 = 8000 \div ....$

Cheaper fish — now that's what I call Plaice Value...

Place value is really important for our number system. It's how we get away with only having ten different digits. If you don't understand anything on this page, don't go **ANY** further in the book. Make sure you can understand it **PROPERLY**. I mean it — it'll be worth it in the long run.

Place Value and Ordering

Q1   Put these numbers in order, from the smallest to the largest.

a)   1.54   1.71   1.98   1.3   1.89   1.5   1.62

b)   102.8   101.2   100.3   102.89   100.4   101.6   100.43

c)   4   0   -1   -10   2   5   -3

d)   7.41   7.36   7.13   7.09   7.40   7.18   7.21

Q2   Put these measurements in descending order.

a)   4.0 cm   4.1 cm   2.3 cm   3.1 cm   2 cm   3.9 cm   0.9 cm

b)   76.1 km   79.1 km   74.9 km   74.1 km   75.2 km   78.7 km   74.3 km

c)   0.102 m   0.219 m   0.02 m   0.009 m   0.021 m   0.012 m   0.220 m

d)   40.73 g   40.93 g   40.81 g   41.06 g   40.07 g   41.1 g   40.7 g

Q3   Insert the correct symbol (<, = or >) in the boxes in the following statements.

a)   9.1 ☐ 8.9

b)   0.139 ☐ 0.141

c)   −7 ☐ −4

d)   0.6 ☐ 3/5

e)   107.61 ☐ 106.71

f)   −76.7 ☐ −77.6

Q4   Write a decimal fraction that lies between the following pairs:

a)   3.0 and 3.5

b)   10.4 and 10.7

c)   6.3 and 6.4

d)   3.72 and 3.76

e)   9.21 and 9.22

f)   0.54 and 0.55

I can't find any pears in here...

Q5   Write the number that is halfway between the following pairs:

a)   0.01 and 0.02

b)   4.3 and 4.4

c)   101.7 and 101.8

d)   0.04 and 0.06

e)   3.1 and 3.4

f)   -3.1 and -3.2

Q6   List all the integers (whole numbers) that obey these rules:

a)   7 < ? < 12

b)   102 < ? < 108

c)   223 < ? < 229

d)   23 < ? < 29

Order of the day — learn all of this...

Ideally, what you want to be able to do is order numbers without even thinking about it. So if you see a group of numbers you know the order of them straight away. Unfortunately, there's no magic way to do this — it just comes with practice... nothing else. But once it's done, it's done.

Place Value and Ordering

Q1 This table shows the temperatures at midnight and midday in six cities around the world. Find the missing values *a-e*.

	City	Temperature at Midnight (°C)	Temperature at Midday (°C)	Temperature rise
	Barcelona	5	12	7
a)	Calgary	-22	-12	a
b)	Lima	b	26	12
c)	Singapore	22	c	9
d)	Moscow	-15	-7	d
e)	London	-1	e	7

Q2 Eileen is using the lift because she is bored. Which floors does she visit?

a) Starts on ground level. She then goes up 7 floors and down 3 floors.

b) Starts on the third floor. She then goes up 7 floors and down 4 floors.

c) Starts in the basement and then goes up 8 floors and down 7.

d) Starts on floor 5, goes down 2, up 6, and then down 10.

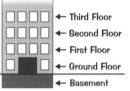

← Third Floor
← Second Floor
← First Floor
← Ground Floor
← Basement

Q3 Chris has trouble with his money. Work out how much he owes or has left at the end when:

a) He owes his mum £4. He reduces his debt by £3.50 by washing her car.

b) He has £4.50. He buys a £9.25 book by borrowing the rest.

c) He has 50p, gets £28 for his birthday and buys 2 CDs for £13.50 each.

Q4 The Dead Sea is 400 m below sea level. Lake Titicaca is 3810 m above sea level. What is the height difference between them?

Q5 Shane has a younger brother called Henry. Shane is 3 years older than Henry. Give 3 possible ages for Shane and Henry.

Q6 Complete these three magic squares.

?	2	-6
?	?	?
0	-8	-1

-5	?	?
?	-2	-3
0	?	1

?	4	0
?	-1	?
-2	-6	?

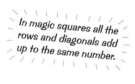

In magic squares all the rows and diagonals add up to the same number.

One boy band and another — what's the difference...

The stuff on this page is pretty useful — you won't hear that often about a page of maths. You'll always be having to work out the difference between things — make sure you can do it now.

4

Place Value, Ordering and Rounding

Q1 Round these figures to: (i) 2 decimal places; (ii) 1 decimal place; (iii) nearest whole number

   a) 6.128   c) 0.063   e) 0.981

   b) 5.914   d) 11.959   f) 1.198

Round the numbers very roughly —just so you get some idea of the answer

Q2 For each sum, check which of the four answers is correct by rounding.

   a) 3.1 × 9.7 = *3 × 10 = 30*   300.7   (30.07)   0.3007   3.007

   b) 53 × 72 =   381.6   38.16   3816   38160

   c) 1169 ÷ 14 =   8350   8.35   0.835   83.5

   d) 0.09 × 442 =   3.978   39.78   397.8   0.3978

   e) 17.28 ÷ 2.7 =   640   64   6.4   0.64

   f) 0.9 × 0.06 =   0.54   5.4   0.054   0.0054

Q3 Wayne is an overweight ping-ponger. His coach decides to weigh him. He used to weigh 62 kg, but now he is 2.9 times heavier.

Estimate Wayne's mass. Show your working

Q4 Derek is buying food and drink for his sister's party. There will be 25 children at the party. What is the minimum number of each item/thing he has to buy so that everyone has at least one of everything?

REMEMBER - there must be enough for everyone

   a) Multi-packs of crisps (15 bags in each pack).

   b) Bottles of cola. Each person will want 3 glasses — 1 bottle contains enough for 10 glasses.

   c) Sausage rolls — these are sold in packs of 4.

   d) Chocolate bars — these are sold in packs of 9.

   e) Mum gives Derek and his friends all the unused food. What did they have?

Q5 Lucy's bedroom is 3.7 m long and 3.9 m wide. She is going to buy carpet tiles for the floor which are 50 cm square. How many will she need?

Hint: It might help to make a sketch

Five is the magic number...

Five is the one to remember. If you're rounding to the <u>nearest ten</u>, then when you get to five you <u>round up</u>. That's it really. Everything else is dead obvious. So don't be lazy and learn about five.

Section One — Numbers and the Number System

Properties of Numbers

Q1   Match each number below to its equal.

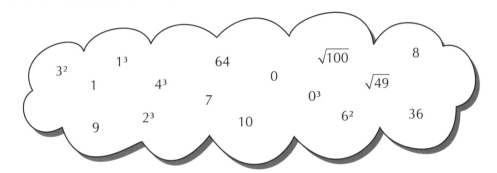

Q2   Copy and complete the following. The first one has been done for you.

a) $\sqrt{3.9}$ is a number between 1 and 2 ←

Because √1 = 1 and √4 = 2

b) $\sqrt{10.5}$ is a number between ..... and .....

c) $\sqrt{6.4}$ is a number between ..... and ......

Q3   Use your calculator to work out these:

a) 13^2 e) 1.3^2

b) $\sqrt{289}$ f) $\sqrt{10}$ (round to 1 d.p.)

c) 0.2^3 g) 199^2

d) 1.9^3 h) $\sqrt{59}$ (round to 1 d.p.)

Q4   Write out the square numbers up to 13^2. Find two square numbers that add up to make another square number.

Q5   Here is a number pattern (called the triangular numbers).

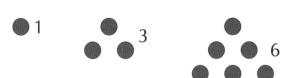

a)   Draw the next three pictures in the pattern.

b)   How many dots will there be on the bottom row of the
(i) 3rd shape;   (ii) 5th shape;   (iii) 25th shape?

c)   Add any two consecutive triangle numbers together. What do you notice?

Properties of Numbers

Q1 Write down all the prime numbers up to 30.

Q2 Write down all the factors of these numbers:

a) 10   d) 48   g) 70

b) 28   e) 72   h) 42

c) 7   f) 25   i) 180

I is a factor of *every* number

Q3 What is the highest common factor (HCF) of:

a) 25 and 70   c) 48 and 28

b) 28 and 42   d) 72 and 180

Use your answers from Q2 to help.

What a lovely sieve I have...

Q4 What is the lowest common multiple (LCM) of:

a) 3 and 8   c) 6 and 9

b) 8 and 12   d) 18 and 24

USING THE SIEVE OF ERATOSTHENES
1. Find or draw a 10x10 grid.
2. Colour in the multiples of 2 (that are greater than 2).
3. Colour in the multiples of 3 (that are greater than 3).
4. Colour in the multiples of the next number that's not itself coloured in.
5. Keep doing this for all numbers up to 100.

Q5 Use the sieve of Eratosthenes to find the primes to 100.

Q6 Each phrase below correctly describes one number only. Write down each number.

a) An odd factor of 14 greater than 1

b) A common factor of 36 and 60 with 2 digits

c) The lowest common multiple of 10 and 16

d) The largest odd factor of 18

e) The smallest common factor of 16 and 24 but not 1

f) The highest common factor of 8, 28 and 60

Q7 Fill in the blanks in these multiplication tables. The first table has been completed for you.

✕	3	8
7	21	56
5	15	40

✕		
	12	6
	66	33

✕		
	24	108
	32	144

Factors — common have a go...

There are a few terms you've got to learn on this page. Like Highest Common Factor (HCF), and Lowest Common Multiple (LCM). Make sure you know what they are and how you can find them.

Properties of Numbers

Q1   Write:

a) $3 \times 3 \times 3 \times 3$ as a power of 3

b) $4 \times 4 \times 4 \times 4 \times 4$ as a power of 4

c) $10 \times 10 \times 10 \times 10 \times 10 \times 10 \times 10$ as a power of 10

d) 25×25 as a power of 25

Q2   Write:

a)   8 as a power of 2   d)   16 as a power of 2

b)   27 as a power of 3   e)   1000 as a power of 10

c)   16 as a power of 4   f)   125 as a power of 5

Q3   Write each of the following numbers as a product of prime numbers:

a)   12   d)   75   g)   54

b)   36   e)   126   h)   100

c)   42   f)   44

Q4   Write each of the answers to Question 3 in index form.

Q5   Join up the numbers that are the same. One has been done for you.

10^2 10^3 1000000 10^1 100000

10   100   1000 10^6 10^5

Q6   Jessica Honeytum has 10 sweet jars with 100 sweets in each one. How many
sweets does she have in total? Write your answer in index form using powers of 10.

Q7   If 10,000 fans attend each of Scumchester United's football games, how many
tickets will be sold after 10 weeks? Write your answer as a power of 10.

What did the German mathematician say? — 3^2 ...

Get your head round index form — it's dead useful when you want to write really big numbers.
Like a million million million million million million million million million million million millions (10^{72}).

Fractions

Q1 Fill in the blanks in these equivalent fractions:

a) 1/2 = ☐/6 = ☐/12 = 2/☐ = ☐/40 = ☐/100 = 250/☐

b) 1/3 = ☐/12 = 3/☐ = ☐/90 = ☐/21 = 10/☐ = ☐/900

c) 1/5 = ☐/10 = ☐/100 = 4/☐ = ☐/35 = ☐/200 = 100/☐

d) 3/7 = 6/☐ = ☐/21 = ☐/49 = 12/☐ = 60/☐ = ☐/350

Q2 Reduce these fractions to their lowest terms:

a) $\frac{3}{9}$ c) $\frac{28}{35}$ e) $\frac{1500}{3500}$

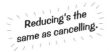
Reducing's the same as cancelling.

b) $\frac{50}{200}$ d) $\frac{28}{63}$ f) $\frac{237}{2370}$

Q3 Change these improper fractions to mixed fractions:

a) $\frac{5}{2}$ c) $\frac{15}{7}$ e) $\frac{9}{4}$

b) $\frac{35}{10}$ d) $\frac{15}{6}$ f) $\frac{18}{5}$

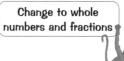
Change to whole numbers and fractions

Q4 Change these to improper fractions:

a) $2\frac{1}{2}$ c) $3\frac{1}{5}$ e) $5\frac{3}{10}$

b) $1\frac{1}{4}$ d) $2\frac{2}{7}$ f) $4\frac{3}{8}$

Q5 Mark the position of these fractions on a number line like this one:

a) $\frac{1}{3}$ c) $\frac{3}{4}$ e) $\frac{9}{10}$

b) $\frac{5}{8}$ d) $\frac{2}{5}$ f) $\frac{1}{10}$

Q6 Noreen and Norma share a packet of 20 sweets, Noreen has 3/5 of the packet, Norma has 1/4. They give the rest to Norman. How many sweets do they have each?

Q7 Boris loves to eat. He tries to eat as much as he can, whenever he can. Do you think Boris would rather have 3/4 of a pizza or 5/8 of a pizza ? Give reasons for your answer.

Learn your fractions — no half measures...

It's a good idea to know how big some of the most common fractions are. Like 2/3 is bigger than 1/2 but smaller than 3/4. Reducing fractions to their lowest terms is also pretty essential. Do it.

Converting Fractions

Q1 Convert these fractions to decimals.

a) $\dfrac{1}{2}$ d) $\dfrac{1}{16}$ g) $\dfrac{1}{10}$

b) $\dfrac{1}{4}$ e) $\dfrac{3}{4}$ h) $\dfrac{3}{10}$

c) $\dfrac{1}{8}$ *Hint: 1/8 is a half of 1/4*   f) $\dfrac{3}{8}$ i) $\dfrac{3}{20}$

Q2 Complete these equations converting fractions to decimals *(the first one's been done for you)*.

a) $\dfrac{1}{2} = \dfrac{5}{10} = \boxed{0.5}$ d) $\dfrac{2}{5} = \dfrac{\ }{10} = \square$ g) $\dfrac{7}{50} = \dfrac{\ }{100} = \square$

b) $\dfrac{1}{4} = \dfrac{\ }{100} = \square$ e) $\dfrac{3}{20} = \dfrac{\ }{100} = \square$ h) $\dfrac{39}{50} = \dfrac{\ }{100} = \square$

c) $\dfrac{1}{5} = \dfrac{\ }{10} = \square$ f) $\dfrac{3}{25} = \dfrac{\ }{100} = \square$ i) $\dfrac{13}{25} = \dfrac{\ }{100} = \square$

Q3 Convert these fractions to percentages.

a) $\dfrac{1}{2}$ c) $\dfrac{3}{4}$ e) $\dfrac{3}{20}$ g) $\dfrac{3}{25}$

b) $\dfrac{1}{4}$ d) $\dfrac{3}{10}$ f) $\dfrac{4}{5}$ h) $\dfrac{7}{25}$

Q4 Change these percentages to decimals and then to fractions.

a) 10%   c) 25%   e) 70%   g) 150%

b) 20%   d) 30%   f) 80%   h) 225%

Q5 Use a calculator to convert these to decimals. Give your answer to 3 d.p. where appropriate.

a) $\dfrac{1}{8}$ c) $\dfrac{1}{7}$ e) $\dfrac{29}{200}$ g) $\dfrac{1}{3}$

b) $\dfrac{3}{16}$ d) $\dfrac{3}{11}$ f) $\dfrac{23}{200}$ h) $\dfrac{2}{3}$

Q6 Convert $\frac{1}{9}$, $\frac{2}{9}$, $\frac{3}{9}$ to decimals. Notice any patterns or anything?

This page'd make a great paper aeroplane...

Remember the FDP (Fraction-Decimal-Percentage) method and you can't possibly go wrong (probably). Divide the fraction to get the decimal, and then times by 100 to get a percentage.

Ordering Fractions

Q1 Put these fractions in ascending order.

a) $\dfrac{1}{2}$ $\quad$ $\dfrac{1}{4}$ $\quad$ $\dfrac{3}{4}$ $\quad$ $\dfrac{5}{8}$ $\quad$ $\dfrac{3}{8}$

d) $\dfrac{4}{5}$ $\quad$ $\dfrac{1}{2}$ $\quad$ $\dfrac{5}{6}$ $\quad$ $\dfrac{2}{3}$ $\quad$ $\dfrac{3}{4}$

b) $\dfrac{1}{16}$ $\quad$ $\dfrac{3}{8}$ $\quad$ $\dfrac{3}{16}$ $\quad$ $\dfrac{5}{8}$ $\quad$ $\dfrac{3}{4}$ $\quad$ $\dfrac{15}{16}$

e) $\dfrac{1}{100}$ $\quad$ $\dfrac{1}{50}$ $\quad$ $\dfrac{3}{25}$ $\quad$ $\dfrac{7}{100}$ $\quad$ $\dfrac{3}{10}$

c) $\dfrac{1}{3}$ $\quad$ $\dfrac{1}{6}$ $\quad$ $\dfrac{5}{6}$ $\quad$ $\dfrac{2}{3}$ $\quad$ $\dfrac{1}{2}$ $\quad$ 1

f) $\dfrac{77}{100}$ $\quad$ $\dfrac{39}{50}$ $\quad$ $\dfrac{19}{25}$ $\quad$ $\dfrac{23}{25}$

Q2 Write a fraction that lies between each of these pairs of numbers.

a) $\dfrac{1}{4}$ and $\dfrac{1}{2}$

d) $\dfrac{1}{3}$ and $\dfrac{2}{3}$

g) $\dfrac{4}{50}$ and $\dfrac{1}{10}$

b) 0 and $\dfrac{1}{3}$

e) $\dfrac{5}{8}$ and $\dfrac{3}{4}$

h) 0.7 and 0.8

c) $\dfrac{4}{5}$ and 1

f) $\dfrac{4}{10}$ and $\dfrac{1}{2}$

Q3 Here are groups of three numbers. For each group, put the numbers in descending order.

a) $\dfrac{7}{10}$ $\qquad$ 50% $\qquad$ 0.4

e) 0.11 $\qquad$ 10% $\qquad$ $\dfrac{1}{11}$

b) 80% $\qquad$ $\dfrac{3}{5}$ $\qquad$ 0.7

f) $\dfrac{1}{3}$ $\qquad$ 33% $\qquad$ 0.04

c) 35% $\qquad$ $\dfrac{9}{20}$ $\qquad$ 0.33

g) 4% $\qquad$ $\dfrac{4}{10}$ $\qquad$ 0.39

d) 0.91 $\qquad$ 99% $\qquad$ $\dfrac{9}{10}$

h) $\dfrac{13}{25}$ $\qquad$ 53.5% $\qquad$ 0.531

Q4 Look at the numbers on the right. Put them into four sets of three equal numbers.

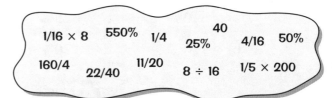

1/16 × 8 $\quad$ 550% $\quad$ 1/4 $\quad$ 40 $\quad$ 25% $\quad$ 4/16 $\quad$ 50%
160/4 $\quad$ 22/40 $\quad$ 11/20 $\quad$ 8 ÷ 16 $\quad$ 1/5 × 200

Q5 Great Aunt Isobel is making her will. She decides to leave $\dfrac{1}{4}$ of her fortune to Jock, $\dfrac{3}{8}$ to Jimmy and the rest to the Loch Ness Monster Protection League. She leaves £1500 to Jock.

a) How much does Jimmy inherit?

b) What is left for Nessie?

Q6 Derek, Dwayne, Rita and Pearl are sharing a Stoneage Superbar. Derek takes $\dfrac{1}{4}$, Rita takes $\dfrac{3}{8}$ and Pearl takes $\dfrac{3}{16}$. How much is left for Dwayne?

Fractions of Shapes and Quantities

Q1 What fraction of each of these shapes is shaded?

a)
c)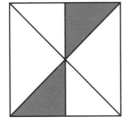
e)

b)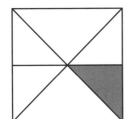
d)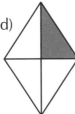
f)

Q2 What fraction of each of these shapes is shaded?

a)
b)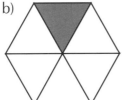
c)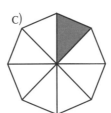
d)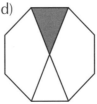
e)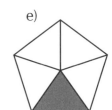

Q3 Draw three rectangles, 2 cm by 3 cm, and label them A, B and C.

a) Shade an area $\frac{3}{8}$ of A.

b) Shade an area $\frac{5}{6}$ of B.

c) Shade an area $\frac{3}{16}$ of C.

Q4 Find:

a) 1/4 of 8 m.

b) 1/10 of 340 kg.

c) 1/9 of £36.

d) 4 × 1/8.

e) 16 × 0.2.

f) £27 ÷ 9.

Fractions of Numbers and Quantities

Q1   Use an arrow to join equal quantities.

50% of 8   10% of 50 $\frac{1}{3}$ of 57   810 ÷ 9   72 × $\frac{1}{6}$

0.25 × 76   1% of 200   10% of 120   16 × $\frac{1}{8}$

40% of 200   450 × $\frac{1}{5}$ 32 ÷ 8   0.2 × 400 $\frac{1}{5}$ of 25

Q2   Work out these percentages in your head.

a)   50% of 400   e)   20% of 25

b)   25% of 200   f)   75% of 12

c)   10% of 250   g)   80% of 10

d)   1% of 600   h)   15% of 240

Q3   Work these out without using your calculator.

a)   10% of £34   e)   60% of 1m

b)   10% of £5   f)   60% of 1 cm

c)   5% of £1   g)   50% of 1 km

d)   5% of £15   h)   5% of 1 km

Q4   Use your calculator to find these values:

a)   12% of £54.20   e)   28% of £100.80

b)   21% of 43 m   f)   62% of 1 kg

c)   2/3 of £66.66   g)   51% of £84.20

d)   3/8 of 54 kg   h)   91% of 540 g

Give your answers to a sensible degree of accuracy

Q5   Mr Stone is paying Aisha to clean his cars. Aisha will be paid (in £), either 25% of the house number or 3 times the number of vehicles. Which should she choose?

Fractions, Percentages, Decimals — all taste the same with gravy...

You can't go wrong if you remember the two "idiot-proof" rules — "%" means "÷ 100", and "of" means "multiply". It's just a different way of writing the same thing — like most maths.

<u>Proportion</u>

Q1   For each of these shapes:

   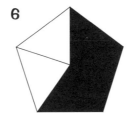   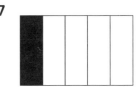

a)   Work out the fraction shaded black and the fraction shaded white.

b)   Write the answers from part a) as decimal fractions.

c)   Convert your answers from part a) to percentages.

d)   Write the ratio of white to black in each shape.

Q2   In the zoo there are three times as many Dodos as there are Woolly Mammoths. If there are six Mammoths how many Dodos are there?

Q3   The number of Yetis is 1/10 of the number of Swamp Things. If there are 20 Swamp Things how many Yetis are there?

Q4   There are 5 velociraptors to every 3 triceratops. If there are 9 triceratops how many velociraptors are there?

Q5   In the zoo cafe they sell "Jungle Juice". To make 1 litre of Jungle Juice requires 3 oranges, 1 mango and 2 peaches. The staff estimate they will need 20 litres. How much fruit do they need to buy?

Q6   In each "swamp sandwich" the cafe puts 1 egg and 1½ tomatoes.

a)   How many sandwiches can be made with 12 eggs?

b)   How many sandwiches can be made with 9 tomatoes?

c)   One morning there are 25 eggs and 36 tomatoes. How many sandwiches can be made? What will be left over?

Ratio

Q1 Express these ratios in their simplest form:

a) 2:4

b) 3:9

c) 20:30

d) 45:90

e) 20:80

f) 16:2

g) 21:7

h) 5:25

Q2 Divide each amount in the ratio given:

a) £8 in ratio 1:1

b) £6 in ratio 1:2

c) £12 in ratio 1:3

d) £24 in ratio 5:1

e) £100 in ratio 4:1

f) £100 in ratio 1:3

g) £1.50 in ratio 2:1

h) £24 in ratio 1:7

Q3 In a wood there are oak trees and beech trees in the ratio 1:4.

a) In the wood there are 100 oak trees. How many beech trees are there?

b) How many trees are there altogether?

c) 200 trees are cut down by a crazy axeman. How many would you expect to be oaks?

Q4 a) In Kieran's class there are 14 girls and 12 boys. Write the ratio of boys to girls in its simplest form.

b) In Gordon's class the ratio of girls to boys is 4:5. If there are 12 girls, how many children are in the class altogether?

c) In Charlotte's Greek class there are 3 boys and 4 girls. What is the ratio of boys to girls?

d) Gavin arrives. What happens to the ratio now?

e) Cherry's in a class with has 22 boys and 10 girls. What is the ratio of boys to girls and the ratio of girls to boys?

Q5 There are 6 T-Rexs, 3 Brontosaurs and 3 Raptors at the zoo.

a) What is the ratio of Brontosaurs to Raptors?

b) What is the ratio of Brontosaurs to T-Rexs?

c) What is the ratio of Raptors : total animals?

Ratio, ratio — wherefore art thou ratio...

Always, always, always add up the numbers in the ratio to get the total number of parts — then find out what one part is.....sound familiar? Do them over and over until you get them all right.

Multiplication and Division

Multiplication and division are <u>mega-important</u> — you've <u>got</u> to get to grips with them.

Q1   Work out these multiplications using some kind of shortcut method:

a)   16 × 9 =   d)   23 × 99 =

b)   15 × 18 =   e)   123 × 29 =

c)   43 × 19 =   f)   123 × 2.9 =

> *A few shortcut methods* (in case you've forgotten them all)*:*
> *a number × 9 = (that number × 10) – (that number × 1)*
> *a number × 15 = (that number × 10) + (that number × 5)*
> *and so on...*

Q2   Match up the pairs which have the same value, by putting a ring round each pair.

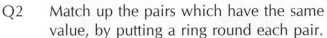
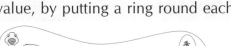

a)   (3 + 2) × 2   d)   (6 ÷ 3) × 5

b)   (5 + 4) × 2   e)   (10 ÷ 2) × 3

c)   3 × (2 + 3)   f)   3 × (2 + 4)

Q3   Work these out in your head:

a)   4 × 11 × 5   c)   2 × 7 × 5 × 5   e) $\frac{1}{2} \times \frac{1}{4} \times 4 \times 10$

b)   7 × 2 × 7   d)   8 × 4 × 5 × 2   f) $8 \times 3 \times 5 \times \frac{1}{4}$

Q4   Work out each division and write down one corresponding multiplication fact.

a)   112 ÷ 8   c)   378 ÷ 21   e) $\frac{204}{17}$

b)   210 ÷ 14   d)   1071 ÷ 21   f)   2400/15

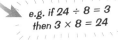

> *e.g. if 24 ÷ 8 = 3*
> *then 3 × 8 = 24*

Q5   Work out these sums. Write each answer in three ways:
(i) number + remainder
(ii) fraction
(iii) decimal fraction (to 2 decimal places).

> *eg: (i) 23 ÷ 2 = 11 remainder 1*
> *(ii) 23 ÷ 2 = 11 $\frac{1}{2}$*
> *(iii) 23 ÷ 2 = 11.5*

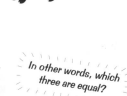

a)   25 ÷ 4 =   c)   91 ÷ 8 =   e)   91 ÷ 6 =

b)   63 ÷ 12 =   d)   404 ÷ 40 =   f)   67 ÷ 3 =

Q6   Three of these expressions have the same value. Which are they?

> *In other words, which three are equal?*

① $\frac{1}{4}$ of 12.8   ② $\frac{1}{5} \times 17$ ③ $25.6 \times \frac{1}{8}$ ④ $19.2 \div 6$ ⑤ $21.7 \times \frac{1}{7}$

Q7   Joe has 626 pickled onions in a jar. If he shares them between the six members of his family how many will each person get?

Corresponding Divisions — sounds like the army...

I can't stress this enough — <u>*MULTIPLICATION AND DIVISION ARE MEGA-IMPORTANT*</u>. You should be able to do all the stuff on this page — if you got <u>any wrong</u>, go back and <u>do them again</u>.

When and How to Multiply and Divide

Q1 Work out the following:

a) $4 + 3 \times 6$

b) $(4 + 3) \times 6$

c) $(24 + 36) \div (4 + 2)$

d) $24 + \frac{36}{4} + 2$

e) $24 + 36 \div (4 + 2)$

f) $(3 + 9)^2 \div 4$

g) $(3 + 9^2) \div 4$

h) $3 + 9^2 \div 4$

i) $(3 + 9) \div 4^2$

Q2 Thelma has 33 beans to sell. How many tins will she have to sell if each tin holds:

a) 6 beans

b) 8 beans

c) 10 beans

d) 9 beans

Q3 Englebert has picked 148 lemons from his tree and is putting them in bags. How many bags will he have to sell, and how many lemons will be left for him to eat if:

a) each bag holds 12 lemons?

b) each bag holds 8 lemons?

c) each bag holds 10 lemons?

d) each bag holds 20 lemons?

Q4 On her birthday Delilah has £75 to take her friends bowling. How many people can go if bowling costs:

a) £5 per person?

b) £8 per person?

c) £11 per person?

d) £12.50 per person?

Q5 Mr Maguh is organising the transport for a school trip. There are 632 children going on the trip. How many buses will be needed if:

a) Each bus can carry 50 people?

b) Each bus can carry 75 people?

c) Each bus can carry 64 people?

d) Each bus can carry 70 people?

e) Mr Maguh then decides that each bus must have two teachers to spoil the fun. How many buses will he need if each carries 60 people?

Q6 Use a calculator for the following questions. Make sure your answer is sensible.

a) £43,189 ÷ 3

b) 1546 kg ÷ 7

c) 5 m ÷ 500

d) 10 pizzas shared between 16 people

e) 568 sweets shared between 53 monkeys

f) 3 hours ÷ 9

Get those brackets sorted (or your shelves will fall down)

Brackets — look there's no big mystery here. You need to work out what's <u>inside the bracket</u> first, before you do anything else. Remember: *3 × (1+2)* is **NOT** the same as *3×1 + 2.*

Mental Methods — Addition and Subtraction

Q1   Find the missing numbers.

a) $46 + ? = 100$ d) $0.7 + ? = 1$ g) $1.3 + ? = 10$

b) $71 = ? = 100$ e) $? + 0.4 = 1$ h) $? + 7.7 = 10$

c) $? + 67 = 100$ f) $0.82 + ? = 1$ i) $94.5 + ? = 100$

Q2   Work out these.

a)   Double 640   d)   Half of 334.6   g)   Half of 48 890

b)   Double 43.6   e)   Double 2350   h)   Half of 2360

c)   Half of 1240   f)   Double 580   i)   Double 986

Q3   More missing numbers to find.

a) $4 \times \boxed{} = 6^2$ c) $39 + \boxed{} = 7^2$ e) $4^2 = 2 \times \boxed{}$ g) $5 \times \boxed{} = 10^2$

b) $19 + \boxed{} = 5^2$ d) $8^2 = 39 + \boxed{}$ f) $36 \times \boxed{} = 12^2$ h) $11^2 = 10^2 + \boxed{}$

Q4   Work out the values of these powers and roots.

a) $10^2, 1.0^2, 0.1^2$ d) $\sqrt{36}, \sqrt{0.36}, \sqrt{3600}$ g) 3^3

b) $3^2, 30^2, 0.3^2,$ e) $\sqrt{0.16}$ h) 5^3

c) $9^2, 0.9^2, 90^2$ f) $\sqrt{0.64}$ i) $\sqrt[3]{8}$

Q5   Complete this table.

Fraction	1/2	1/4		1/10				1/8		
Decimal			0.2			1.25			0.01	2.1
Percentage	50%				15%		175%			

Q6   Complete these number sentences:

a)   2 hours = ...minutes = ...seconds   e)   5 miles is approximately ....km

b)   1 week = ...days = ...hours   f)   2.5 kg = ...g

c)   3 km = ...m = ...cm   g)   1 kg is approximately ....lb

d)   5.5 m = ...cm = ...mm   h)   1 gallon is approximately ...litres

Mental Methods — Addition and Subtraction

Q1 Try these addition and subtraction sums:

a) 8 + 23   d) 59 + 43   g) 77 + 75

b) 23 + 38   e) 68 + 25   h) 66 – 28

c) 36 + 47   f) 93 – 21   i) 93 – 58

Q2 These are a bit more tricky.

a) 8.8 + 3.1   d) 11.7 – 4.6   g) 0.53 – 0.09

b) 6.9 + 3.5   e) 4.8 + 8.8   h) 3.21 – 1.23

c) 9.3 – 5.4   f) 0.83 + 8.55   i) 7.01 – 6.97

Q3 Work out these calculations:

a) 8 – 4 – 5 + 7 =   e) -3 – 7 – 2 + 12 =

b) – 4 – 7 + 5 – 3 =   f) 120 – 140 + 60 – 40 =

c) – 10 + 23 + 5 – 8 =   g) 800 – 900 – 400 + 200 =

d) 8 – 9 + 12 – 6 =   h) 5000 – 9000 + 3000 =

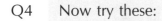
It might help to draw a number line

Q4 Now try these:

a) 72 – 69   d) 4.01 – 3.99

b) 201 – 199   e) 6.01 – 5.98

c) 6.1 – 5.9   f) 0.11 – 0.09

Q5 In a game of darts Will scored 69 with three bird-darts. His first two darts scored 57 and 2. What did he score with his third bird-dart?

Q6 Farzana and Jo are building a wall. Farzana uses 39 stones and Jo uses 45. Then Patch the dog knocks out 10 stones. How many are left in the wall?

Q7 The tree outside Kate's house is 24 m taller than the chimney. The top of the chimney is 2.5 m above the ground. How tall is the tree?

It's tricky — Sumtimes...

Tricks and scribbles is what it's all about. Use tricks like splitting sums (e.g. split "34 – 12" into "34 – 10 = 24" then "24 – 2 = <u>22</u>") and scribble notes to help you remember what you're doing.

Properties of Numbers

Q1 Calculate these without a calculator *(try "counting on")*:

a) 1009 – 998   d) 6432 – 4950   g) 9.06 – 7.90

b) 3247 – 3236   e) 8025 – 7975   h) 0.546 – 0.380

c) 4135 – 3900   f) 7400 – 3750

Q2 Work out the value of these:

a) 78 + 19   d) 546 – 21   g) 3449 + 39

b) 4.5 + 2.9   e) 783 – 29   h) 0.1234 + 0.09

c) 7.2 – 0.9   f) 0.64 + 0.9

> Remember:
> 78 + 19 = 78 + 20 – 1

Q3 These can be worked out using "near doubles":

a) 9.1 + 9.2   e) 4320 + 4325

b) 75 + 74   f) 0.036 + 0.037

c) 0.17 + 0.18   g) 0.19 + 0.17

d) 935 + 936   h) 3.2 + 3.3 + 3.4

Stop! Stop! Sam's exploded.

Q4 Use these number facts to work out the following questions:

> 793 + 1187 = 1980
> 841 – 198 = 643
> 0.0141 – 0.0083 = 0.0058
> 0.097 + 0.083 = 0.18

a) 141 – 83   e) 19.8 – 7.93

b) 7.93 + 11.87   f) 0.0058 + 0.0083

c) 0.18 – 0.097   g) 64.3 + 19.8

d) 8.41 – 1.98   h) 18 – 9.7

Q5 Josephine is shopping and only has £10 to spend.
How many of these items can she take home for tea?

Burgers £4.99   Chips £1.98   Chocolate cake £1.99   Orange squash £1.03

Q6 Daniel has £3. How many of these could he buy and how much change would he get?

Chocolate bar 49p   Bottle of cola 99p   Ice cream 98p   Bag of toffees £1.60

Properties of Numbers

Q1 Calculate:

a) 560×50 e) $3400 \div 50$

b) 50×47 f) $5.5 \div 50$

c) 620×500 g) $860 \div 500$

d) 0.47×50 h) $7.2 \div 50$

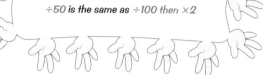

Handy Hints

×50 is the same as ×100 then ÷2

÷50 is the same as ÷100 then ×2

Q2 Now try these:

a) $2.3 \times 12 = (2.3 \times 10) + (2.3 \times 2) =$ e) $12 \times 130 =$

b) $4.3 \times 32 = (4.3 \times ?) + (4.3 \times ?) =$ f) $410 \times 201 =$

c) $7.1 \times 101 =$ g) $23 \times 99 =$

d) $15.3 \times 12 =$ h) $80 \times 99 =$

Remember: 99 = 100 - 1.

Q3 Calculate:

a) $5 \times 27 \times 2$ c) $20 \times 32 \times 5$ e) $25 \times 47 \times 40$ g) $5 \times 0.76 \times 20$

b) $25 \times 7 \times 4$ d) $20 \times 7 \times 5$ f) $50 \times 72 \times 20$ h) $0.4 \times 80 \times 0.1$

Q4 Use these number facts to work out the following questions:

a) 247×3.8 e) $938.6 \div 247$

b) $0.612 \div 3.6$ f) 1.7×3.6

c) 19×3.4 g) $16269 \div 561$

d) 29×56.1 h) $64.6 \div 19$

$247 \times 38 = 9386$

$16269 \div 29 = 561$

$6.46 \div 1.9 = 3.4$

$0.17 \times 3.6 = 0.612$

Q5 Dave and his dad are in Weirdy-Land. They find a huge maggot 2.5 m long which they cut into 8 pieces. How long is each piece of maggot? Give your answer three ways: in metres, centimetres and millimetres.

Counting sheep — that's nothing, I've got a spelling hamster...

Cutting up maggots is a lot like maths... Ok, ok it's not that much like maths, but cutting up sums so they're easier is a good tip. Hint 2: write out word questions as sums before you answer them.

Properties of Numbers

Q1 Finish these number sentences:

a) If $\frac{1}{5}$ = 0.2 then $\frac{4}{5}$ =

e) If $\frac{7}{25}$ = 0.28 then $\frac{14}{25}$ =

b) If 0.1 = $\frac{1}{10}$ then $\frac{7}{10}$ =

f) If $\frac{6}{25}$ = 0.24 then 0.12 =

c) If 0.25 = $\frac{1}{4}$ then $\frac{5}{4}$ =

g) If $\frac{8}{25}$ = 0.32 then $\frac{12}{25}$ =

d) If $\frac{1}{8}$ = 0.125 then $\frac{3}{8}$ =

h) If $\frac{17}{50}$ = 0.34 then $\frac{17}{100}$ =

Q2 Complete this table:

	a)	b)	c)	d)	e)	f)	g)	h)
Decimal		0.15					0.8	
Fraction	27/100			73/100		1/20		170/100
Percentage	27%		45%		120%			

Q3 Work out these fractions and percentages:

a) $\frac{1}{4}$ of 84

e) $32 \times \frac{3}{8}$

b) 50% of 124

f) 20% of 125

c) 80% of 5

g) $\frac{4}{5}$ of 40

d) $\frac{3}{5}$ of 55

h) 75% of 200

Q4 Mehdi is sharing out some change with his sons. He has £7.20 and gives Farzana $\frac{1}{4}$, Ahmed $\frac{1}{3}$ and Tariq $\frac{1}{10}$. He keeps the rest. How much do they each have to spend?

Q5 Harry Belliwell talks three times as much rubbish as a normal person. When asked for eight fractions he gives twenty-four — eight lots of three equal fractions. Find the equal fractions.

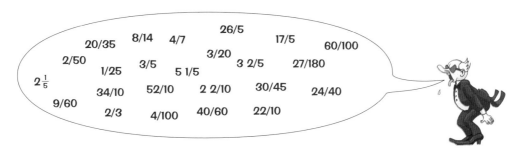

Speech bubble contents:
26/5   17/5
20/35   8/14   4/7   60/100
2/50   3/20   3 2/5   27/180
1/25   3/5   5 1/5
2 1/5   34/10   52/10   2 2/10   30/45   24/40
9/60   2/3   4/100   40/60   22/10

It's no good — my days as a calendar are numbered...

Getting a decimal value from a fraction is dead easy — all you've got to do is divide the top number in the fraction by the bottom number (e.g. ¼ = 1 ÷ 4 = 0.25). Simple as 1, 2, 3½.

Fractions

Q1   Some schoolkids are trying to earn some money in their school holidays. Their charges are listed on the right. How much do they each earn if they do these jobs listed below? Who earns most? Who earns least?

a)   Kate walks four dogs

b)   Leroy washes 1 car and cleans 1 lot of windows

c)   Jo walks 1 dog every day for a week

d)   Will mows 3 lawns

e)   Fran washes 3 cars

f)   Tariq cleans 4 lots of windows

> Car washing £4.50
> Window cleaning £5.30
> Washing up £1.50
> Walking a dog £2.60
> Lawn mowing £6.25

Mmmmm... Honey...

Q2   The children then spend their wages. How much do they spend?

a)   Kate: one 30p chocolate bar every day for 3 weeks

b)   Will: two 20p oranges a day for 2 weeks

c)   Jo: one £3.20 jar of honey every week for 5 weeks

d)   Fran: one 26p icecream every day for 3 weeks

e)   Leroy: one 21p can of cola every day for 1 week

f)   Tariq: three burgers costing £2.99 each

Q3   Use the numbers 4, 6, and 7 to complete these calculations:

a) (_ + _) – _ = 9   e) (_ – _) × _ = 18

b) (_ × _) + _ = 46   f) _ × _ × _ = 168

c) _ × (_ + _) = 70   g) _ – _ – _ = -3

d) (_ + _) × _ = 52   h) _ × _ ÷ _ = 10.5

Q4   Fill in these factor triangles. The numbers on each side of the triangle multiply together to make the number in the centre.

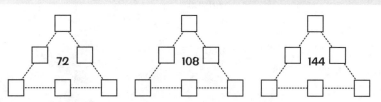

72   108   144

Why did she leave me?

Fractions — and that's not the half of it...

Wordy questions like the first two on this page always come up in maths — they're a way of showing how maths can be used in the real world. It's not fun, but it's got to be done, OK.

Written Methods

Q1 Use a pencil and paper to work out these calculations:

a) 1279 + 334

b) 4796 + 209

c) 569 − 491

d) 243 + 694 + 101

e) 3712 + 1319 + 2240

f) 7348 − 69

g) 1234 + 567 + 89

h) 9876 + 543 + 21

Q2 Try these multiplications:

a) 234 × 63

b) 127 × 36

c) 491 × 16

d) 282 × 27

e) 43 × 311

f) 726 × 42

g) 909 × 52

h) 333 × 33

NO calculators on this page.

Q3 Have a go at these ones too.

a) 1.23 × 34

b) 7.09 × 34

c) 2.36 × 4.2

d) 4.91 × 2.2

e) 6.46 × 0.22

f) 14.6 × 5.3

g) 8.21 × 8.7

h) 34.7 × 1.8

Q4 Mr Dewdrop is clearing up his shop at the end of the day. Work out how much money he earned from selling:

a) 4 planes

b) 23 stickers

c) 13 footballs

d) 11 skateboards

e) 16 books

f) 63 pickled eyeballs

g) 4 kites

h) How much money did he take in total?

Write — No more calculators...

You're not allowed to use calculators on this page. And that's not cos I've got anything against them — it's just that far away in the future (well, at the end of Year 9, anyway) you'll get non-calculator exams. And in your GCSEs. So if you put off doing stuff without calculators you're a duffer.

Section Two — Calculations

Written Methods

Q1 A local company holds a lottery each week. More than one person can win, and the number of tickets sold varies each week. How much money does each person get if the prize money is:

That Guinevere is a generous woman.

a) £56.50 between 10,

b) £101.60 between 4,

c) £252.64 between 8,

d) £96.25 between 5,

e) £169.20 between 3,

f) £1384.00 between 40,

g) £5010.00 between 60,

h) £371.25 between 9?

Q2 Calculate:

a) 322 ÷ 14

b) 357 ÷ 21

c) 651 ÷ 31

d) 1127 ÷ 23

e) 561 ÷ 17

f) 2499 ÷ 49

g) 957 ÷ 33

h) 2142 ÷ 51

Q3 Give these answers as whole number and remainder.

a) 729 ÷ 13

b) 417 ÷ 18

c) 724 ÷ 23

d) 975 ÷ 51

e) 383 ÷ 33

f) 207 ÷ 65

g) 574 ÷ 44

h) 858 ÷ 71

Q4 Give these answers correct to 1 decimal place.

a) 849 ÷ 41

b) 734 ÷ 32

c) 641 ÷ 26

d) 564 ÷ 18

e) 491 ÷ 13

f) 210 ÷ 23

g) 343 ÷ 58

h) 999 ÷ 36

Q5 Mary's Marshmallows are taking people on tours of their amazing factory. Work out how many of each vehicle will be needed.

a) 320 people on buses seating 48

b) 106 people on minibuses seating 12

c) 1350 people on planes seating 105

Addition — Bless you... here's a tissue...

These are pretty hard considering you can't use a calculator. But if you're struggling, there's a sure-fire way to get better at this kind of question — and that's to practise until you can do them.

Calculator Methods

Q1 Work out these:

a) £3.26 × 13   c) £28.33 ÷ 7   e) £200 ÷ 3   g) £4.23 ÷ 8

b) £47.43 × 5   d) £17.45 × 3.5   f) £6.30 ÷ 7   h) £1000 ÷ 3

Give your answer to the nearest penny

Q2 Use your calculator to work out these calculations.
Give your answer in (i) hours and (ii) hours and minutes.

a) 11 hr 30 min × 3   e) 14 hr 30 min ÷ 2

b) 94 hr ÷ 4   f) 1 hr 12 min × 7

c) 100 hr ÷ 8   g) 8 hr ÷ 6

d) 12.5 hr ÷ 2   h) 12 hr ÷ 8

Don't forget there are 60 minutes in an hour

Q3 Use the fraction button to simplify each fraction.

a) $\frac{306}{357}$ c) $\frac{112}{560}$ e) $\frac{405}{324}$ g) $\frac{234}{104}$

b) $\frac{168}{252}$ d) $\frac{138}{230}$ f) $\frac{291}{194}$ h) $\frac{979}{801}$

Q4 Use your fraction button to calculate each sum.

a) $\frac{1}{2} + \frac{5}{7}$ d) $\frac{6}{7} \div \frac{1}{3}$ g) $5\frac{3}{5} \times 4\frac{1}{2}$

b) $\frac{2}{5} - \frac{3}{11}$ e) $1\frac{1}{3} + \frac{5}{6}$ h) $24\frac{1}{8} \times \frac{1}{3}$

c) $\frac{6}{7} \times \frac{1}{3}$ f) $2\frac{7}{8} - \frac{1}{32}$

Q5 Dad won £47.50 in a lobster-eating competition. He divided it between
the three children. Work out how much money each had to spend.

a) He gave Farzana $\frac{8}{15}$ b) He gave Tariq $\frac{2}{10}$ c) He gave Ahmed $\frac{4}{15}$

No. 1: pick up pen — oops, that's writing methods...

I once ate a lobster. Or it might have been a shrimp... can't remember. Anyway, these questions
should be a bit of a doddle if you're any good with calculators — and if you're not, you should be.
Practise these questions until you know exactly what you're doing. There's no excuse not to.

Calculator Methods

Q1   Use your calculator to work out:

a) 21^2 e) $\sqrt{729}$

b) 42.5^2 f) $\sqrt{0.0001}$

c) 0.41^2 g) $3^2 + 4^2$

d) $\sqrt{256}$ h) $11^2 - 6^2$

If only I had a calculator with + and – buttons...

Q2   Use the $+/-$ button on your calculator to solve these.

a) -3×12.5 d) $-3.1 - 7.3$

b) 7.1×-27 e) -2.8×-4.1

c) $-42 \div 3.5$ f) $-86 \div -20$

Q3   Can you work these out mentally using the BODMAS rules?
Write down the keys you use to get the correct result on your calculator.

a) $3 + 4 \times 5$ d) $16 \div 8 + 14 \div 7$ f) $\dfrac{23 - 11}{3 \times 2}$

b) $3 \times 4 + 5$

c) $3 \times 4 - 2 \times 3$ e) $\dfrac{4 + 6}{3 + 1}$

Hint: round all the numbers to 1 sig.fig. first and then do an approximation. That way you'll notice if your answer's wrong.

Q4   These are a bit harder. Can you do them either using the
memory function or the brackets on your calculator?

a) $(45 - 17) \times 3.2$ e) $(11 + 2.6) \div (0.08 + 0.6)$

b) $7.2 \times (8.6 + 1.9)$ f) $(3.4^2 + 4) \times 7$

c) $124 \div (3.4 + 4.6)$ g) $(8.8 + 6.2) \div (11.4 - 1.8) \times (3.4 + 7)$

d) $(23 + 64) \times (2.52 - 1.9)$ h) $(6^2 - 3.4^2) \times \sqrt{5.76}$

Q5   Convert these fractions to decimals (use the dot notation). What do you notice?

a) $\dfrac{1}{9}$,   b) $\dfrac{2}{9}$,   c) $\dfrac{3}{9}$,   d) $\dfrac{4}{9}$

Calculators — better than peanut butter...

Best to be pretty rapid on those calculator buttons — the quicker you can do it, the less work you
have to do. Get your fingers fit by drumming them on your mate's head as fast as you can for ages.

Properties of Numbers

Q1 A class of students were at a pig rodeo. For homework they were set some sums using the times of the rodeo riders.

Here is Will's homework. He's a bit slapdash. Use estimation to check which answers are wrong, then use your calculator to find the correct answer.

a) $3.14 \times 8.2 = 25.748$

b) $67.3 - 31.6 = 3.57$

c) $5.67 - 7.3 \times 3.6 = -5.868$

d) $6.1 + 5.2 \div 2 = 8.7$

e) $65 \times 2 + 5 \times 3 = 1365$

f) $\frac{3+12}{4+1} = 3$

g) $\frac{18-6}{4\times2} = 15$

h) $\frac{21\times3}{3\times3} = 7$

Q2 Here is Jo's homework, check and correct this in the same way.

a) £3.21 + £3.73 = £6.94

b) £8.24 ÷ 4 = £6.02

c) £12.48 + 20p = £32.48

d) £108.99 + 2p = £109.19

e) 9 hr ÷ 6 = 1 hr 50 min

f) 54 000 cm = 540 m

g) 230 m × 6 = 13.8 km

h) 580 g × 9 = 52200 g

Urgh! This is decaf — I want proper tea.

Q3 Calculate the missing numbers in Kate's work.

a) ? + 5.8 = 21.8

b) $\frac{1}{2}$ of ? = 34.5

c) 4.2 × ? = 13.02

d) 789 – ? = 123

e) ? – 43 = 579

f) 56.2 ÷ ? = 22.48

g) ? ÷ $\frac{1}{3}$ = 243

h) (2 + ?) × 3.3 = 16.5

Q4 Mark Tariq's homework and correct the wrong answers.

a) $3.9^2 = 15.21$

b) $\sqrt{8.41} = 2.9$

c) $61^2 = 372.1$

d) $\sqrt{72.25} = 8.5$

e) $\frac{1}{80} = 0.125$

f) $\frac{5}{6} + \frac{7}{8} = \frac{12}{14}$

g) $\frac{1}{2} \div \frac{1}{8} = 4$

h) $3.1^2 + 4.1^2 = 7.2$

If $2^2 = 4$ and $3^2 = 9$ then $\sqrt{2.5}^2$ lies between **4** and **9**

Money, Percentages and Measures

Q1   Stuart is shopping in PC Universe. How much does he spend if he buys:

a)   2 boxes of blank CDs at £16.60 and a computer game for £28?

b)   1 box of blank CDs, 2 packets of paper at £3.50 and 1 printer cartridge at £23.50?

c)   A scanner for £150, 2 packs of paper for £14.50 each and a photo album for £3.00?

Q2   Which is the best value of each of these pairs:

a)   4 computer games at £12.99 or "Buy any 3 at £18, get one free"?

b)   25 floppy discs for £6.00 or 40 for £9.00?

c)   5 CDs for £8.50 or 12 CDs for £21.00?

d)   10 highlighter pens at £3.99 or 4 for £1.70?

e)   Notebooks at 3 for £3.99 or 5 for £6.91?

Wow! This is even better than listening to Radio 4!

Q3   Sarah has bought herself a new laptop costing £1250.
She's also bought a new printer for £150 and a desk for £100.

a)   How much did she spend altogether?

b)   What percentage of her total outlay was the cost of the printer?

c)   What percentage of her total outlay was the cost of the laptop?

d)   The shop had two special offers. Which should she choose?

> *"5% off your total bill" or "Laptop for £1180"*

Q4   Isobel is looking at a photo on her PC screen. The program tells her that she is viewing at 25% of its actual size. If the picture on the screen is 5 cm by 8 cm:

a)   What will be the size of the picture if it is printed at full size?

b)   To save ink she prints it at half width and half length.
What are the dimensions of her print?

c)   What will be the area of the picture when she prints it at this size?

Q5   Stevie is is planning a new shelf for his computer games. He has 35 CDs which are 1 cm thick and 50 DVDs that are 1.6 cm thick. What is the minimum length of shelf that he needs?

Money — I hurt it playing football...

This is the kind of maths I like — working out how to save a bit of cash. Anyway, the hardest thing on this page is probably percentages — and even they're not <u>so</u> bad since there are really only 3 kinds of question they can ask. Learn to do those and you'll have no more percentage worries.

Problems about Ratio and Proportion

Q1   Belle decides to spend her pocket money on sweets, going out and saving in the ratio 2:2:1.

a)   If she gets £15 per week how much will she spend on each?

b)   If she gets a rise to £20 per week how much will she save?

Sweets	:	Going out	:	Saving
2	:	2	:	1

c)   If she gets £20 per week how long will it take to save up for a
computer game that costs £29?

Q2   On a school exchange visit to France, Mary-Jo changes £100 to French Francs.
The exchange rate is £1 = 9 FF. How many Francs will she have to spend?

On her way home Mary-Jo still has 104 FF left. The exchange rate
coming home is 10 FF = £1, how many pounds does she take home?

The State I am in...

Q3   Sebastian is on a trip to Italy. How many Lire will he
get for his £100 if the exchange rate is £1 = 2900 lire?

Q4   Anthony is making cakes to sell at the school disco. Here is a list of
ingredients for Chocolate Brownies. It makes enough for 20 portions.

walnuts: 50g   eggs: 2   cocoa: 40g

butter: 50g   sugar: 225g   flour: 75g

a)   How much of each ingredient will he need to make 120 brownies?

b)   He finds he has only one 200 g tin of cocoa. How many brownies can he make?

Q5   My cat Elvis is tiling the kitchen floor using this pattern:
Each tile is 25 cm × 25 cm. The kitchen is 6 m × 4.5 m.

a)   What is the ratio of blue tiles to white tiles?

b)   How many tiles will he need for the whole floor?

*Hint: divide the floor
into rows and columns*

c)   How many of each colour will he need?

Don't worry about this stuff — get it in proportion...

Ratios look frightening, but they're not really. The ratio 2:3:1 just means you've got 6 'parts'
altogether, and you have to share them out in a certain way. You soon get the hang of them.

Problems about Number and Algebra

Q1 (i) Use the numbers 0 to 9 (use each number no more than once in each question) to make the biggest possible answer. The first one has been done for you.

a) <u>9 8 7 6</u> – <u>0 1</u>   e) _ _ × _ _

b) _ _ _ _ + _ _   f) _ _ _ ÷ _

c) _ _ _ × _   g) _ _ ÷ _ _

d) _ _ _ _ _ × _   h) _ _ _ _ _ + _ _ _ _ _

1	2	3	4	5	6	7	8	9	0

(ii) Now do the same for each part to make the smallest possible answer.

Q2 Fill in the missing signs (+, –, ×, ÷)

a) (430 _ 50) _ 12 = 40   e) (4 _ 6) _ 5 = 50

b) (430 _ 50) _ 19 = 20   f) 4 _ (6 _ 5) = –26

c) (4 _ 6) _ 5 = 19   g) 430 _ (50 _ 12) = 392

d) 4 _ (6 _ 5) = 4   h) 430 _ (50 _ 19) = 361

Q3 What happens to the numbers below when they are put through the number machine on the right? *(The first one has been done for you)*

a) 2 gives 0   c) 4

b) 3   d) 52

What about this machine on the right? Work out what it does to these numbers below.

e) 1   g) 3

f) 2   h) 10

Q4 Now try this machine. What happens to these numbers?

a) 6   c) 8   e) 10

b) 7   d) 9   f) 11

Q5 Describe what these machines have done.

a) Machine A changes 0, 1, 2, 3, 4, into 0, 2, 4, 6, 8

b) Machine B changes 10, 11, 12, 13, 14 into 7, 8, 9, 10, 11

Algebra — it's all gibberish to me...

This page is really about two things: Questions 1 and 2 are about getting your head round numbers and doing things in your head. The other questions are basic algebra — and I love that cos I'm a saddo who spends all my time thinking about maths so I can write books about it for you.

Problems about Number and Algebra

Q1 Work out the perimeter of this kite if:

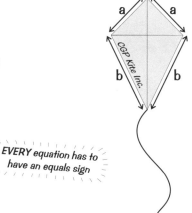

a) $a = 3$ cm; $b = 5$ cm

d) $a = 34$ mm; $b = 3$ cm

b) $a = 3$ m; $b = 10$ m

e) $a = 1.5$ m; $b = 200$ cm

c) $a = 4.1$ cm; $b = 5.9$ cm

Write a general equation for the perimeter P of this kite.

EVERY equation has to have an equals sign

Q2 Write down two consecutive numbers that add up to:

a) 11   c) 31   e) 63   g) 2009

b) 21   d) 41   f) 145

Do any two consecutive numbers add up to an even number? Explain your answer.

Q3 Write down two consecutive ODD numbers that add up to:

a) 20   c) 500   e) 5500

b) 100   d) 1000   f) −4

Eg 3 + 5 = 8

Do two consecutive odd numbers always add up to an even number?

Q4 Dodgy Diana has a dodgy market stall. Her CDs cost £14.50 and audio cassettes cost £7.60.

a) Work out the cost of 2 CDs and 3 cassettes.

b) Write a word equation for the cost, C, of 2 CDs and 3 cassettes.

c) Write an number equation using C, x and y.

Q5 Herman spends all his time buying matchsticks so he can make shapes out of them. A few are shown below. Draw the next one in the series and write down how many matchsticks are needed for the 6th and the 10th pattern in the series.

a) Groups of squares: 4, 7, 10, 13

b) Triangles: 3, 6, 9, 12

c) Christmas trees: 3, 6, 9

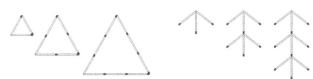

Number — what your hands go in cold weather...

Not many people seem to like algebra — but it's not so bad. You just write 'x' or 'y' instead of something you don't know. Like if a goat costs x and a pig costs y, then a farm costs 10x + 14y.

Problems: Shape, Space, Area and Perimeter

Q1   Work out the missing angles in these shapes:

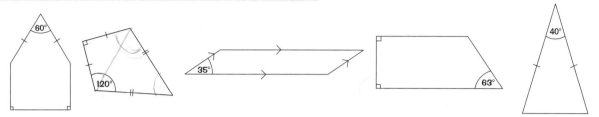

Q2   David and Victoria are putting a path round their garden pond. Their pond is square-shaped with 3 m sides. How many paving stones will they need if:

   a)   the stones are 50 cm square?

   b)   the stones are 75 cm × 75 cm?

   c)   the stones are 25 cm square and they need a path 50 cm wide?

After the path, shall we have a statue like this...?

Q3   Can you draw two DIFFERENT isosceles triangles where one angle only is 50°? Give reasons for your answer.

Where's Alan Titchmarsh when you need him...

Q4   How many squares can you see in each of these shapes?

   a) ☐   b)   c)

Q5   Here is a plan of Brian the monkey's garden.

   a)   What is the area of the whole garden and house?

   b)   What is the area of the flower bed?

   c)   What is the perimeter of the vegetable plot?

   d)   What is the perimeter of the lawn?

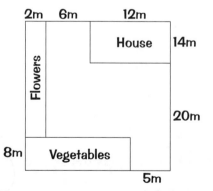

Perimeters — what you call things that eat perim...

With perimeters, you have to make sure you count all of the sides — but only once. I reckon the best way to do that is to put a blob on one of the corners and go round the shape, either clockwise or anticlockwise, writing down the lengths of all the sides until you get back to your blob.

Problems: Shape, Space, Area and Perimeter

Q1 Draw the net for each of these shapes. The first one has been done for you.

a) Triangular pyramid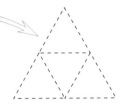

b) Cube

c) Square-based pyramid

d) Cylinder

Who needs nets...

Q2 Draw three DIFFERENT nets for an open-topped box.

Q3 A square has a perimeter of 36 m. What is its area?

Q4 A rectangle has an area of 72 cm² and its length is twice its width. What is its perimeter?

Q5 What is the area shaded in each triangle?

a)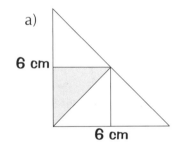

b)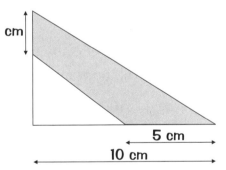

Q6 What fraction of these shapes is shaded? What fraction is unshaded?

a)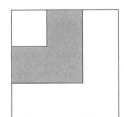

b)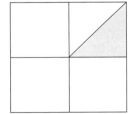

Area — what my bedroom is when I open a window...

The formula for the area of a triangle is a sneaky old devil... after you do the multiplication, you have to remember to divide by 2. If you don't, you get an answer that's well... just plain wrong.

Problems about Probability and Data

Q1 What is the probability of:

a) Getting a six when you roll a die?

b) Getting a seven when you roll a die?

c) The sun rising tomorrow morning?

d) Drawing a card of a red suit from a pack of playing cards?

e) Drawing a three from a pack of playing cards?

f) Getting an even number when you roll a die?

g) Choosing a card with a 1 on it from a set of cards numbered 1 to 20?

h) Choosing a card with a 3 on it from a set of cards numbered 1 to 100?

Q2 Since the local zoo opened there have been 100 attacks on the zookeepers. The animals responsible for the attacks are shown in the bar-chart below. Use the chart to answer these questions.

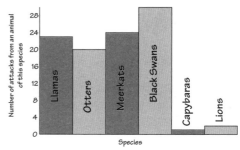

a) What is the probability that the next animal to attack a zookeeper will be an otter?

b) What is the probability that it will be a lion?

c) What is the probability that it will be a black swan or a meerkat?

d) The zoo has to hire a new zookeeper every time the attack is by a lion. How many new zookeepers will they have to hire after:

   (i) 50 animal attacks?   (ii) 100 animal attacks?   (iii) 1000 animal attacks?

e) The local paper charges the zoo £200 to advertise for a new zookeeper. They also pay the zoo £5 for the story every time there is an attack. How much profit does the zoo make from the paper after 100 attacks?

Q3 Fred is playing "Who Wants to Lose a Million Hairs". He's been asked a question and has no idea of the right answer.

a) What is the probability that he will guess correctly if there are five choices of answer?

b) What is the probability that he will get his guess wrong? Give your answers as both a fraction and a decimal.

Getting them all right — what's the chance of that...

Probabilities aren't too tough — remember that nearly always "and" means "multiply" and "or" means "add". If you got any wrong, do them again — drawing little <u>tree diagrams</u> might help.

Using the Right Information

Q1 You have 12 square floor tiles, each with an area of 16 cm².
What arrangement gives (i) the largest perimeter (ii) the smallest perimeter?

Q2 Work out the areas of the following objects:

a) Front door of Penny's dolls' house: 3 cm × 43 mm

b) The footpath in Penny's garden: 5.1 m × 51 cm

c) A road sign: triangle with base 0.4 m, height 550 mm

Q3 Anna is 20, Brian is 10, Clara is 8 and Delores is 2.

a) How many years older than Clara is Anna?

b) When Anna is 26 how old will the others be?

c) How many times older than Delores is Brian?

d) How old will Delores and Brian be in two years time?

e) How many times older than Delores will Brian be then?

Q4 The sequence of numbers below is the first few terms of "The Triangular Number Sequence".

a) How many dots are there in the bottom of the next pattern in the sequence?

b) How many rows are there in the next pattern?

c) How many dots are there in the bottom of the 20th pattern?

d) How many rows are there in the 20th pattern?

Q5 Write down two DIFFERENT sets of calculator key
sequences you could use to calculate each of the following:

With this calculator key sequence I shall take over the world...

a) Half of 45.3.

b) 25% of £84.

c) 3 lots of 56, then subtract 7.3.

d) Profit if you bought 3 toys for £5.50, then sold them for £5.99 each.

e) £79.60 shared between five people.

All I ever really wanted was an hour more in bed...

If you got any of these questions wrong, do them all again....and again....and again. That's the key to maths — loads and loads of practice. Probably why it makes it a bit dull. Still, now you know...

Making Big Problems Small

Q1 Davinia is tidying her bedroom and arranging her books on her bookshelf. Two books can be ordered in two different ways.

a) In how many ways can you order three books?

b) Can you extend the argument for arranging four books on a shelf?

Q2 A book worm eats his way through a set of 10 encyclopaedias. He starts on the front cover and then burrows in the most direct route until he reaches the back cover. If each book is 3 cm thick how many cm has he moved?

Q3 If you have one of every coin in the British currency what different amounts can you make?

There are 1p, 2p, 5p, 10p, 20p, 50p, £1 and £2 coins.

Q4 Here is a rule to generate a sequence of numbers:

"Multiply the previous number by 3 and then subtract 1"

a) Starting with 2 write down the first 5 numbers.

b) Starting with 1 write down the first 5 numbers.

c) Starting with 0 write down the first 5 numbers.

d) Starting with –2 write down the first 5 numbers.

What do you notice about the sequences you've written down?

Q5 Here is another rule to generate a sequence of numbers:

"Take the previous number and square it"

a) Starting with 2 write down the first 5 numbers.

b) Starting with 1 write down the first 5 numbers.

c) Starting with –2 write down the first 5 numbers.

d) Starting with 0.5 write down the first 4 numbers.

e) Starting with 0.1 write down the first 4 numbers.

...and I've got to teach maths to 3B today. Life can't get worse...

You'll need a calculator for this lot.

Presenting the Solution

Q1 Here is part of a 100 number grid. When a 2×2 square is drawn on it you can multiply the numbers in diagonally opposite corners.

1	2	3	4	5	6
11	12	13	14	15	16
21	22	23	24	25	26
31	32	33	34	35	36
41	42	43	44	45	46
51	52	53	54	55	56

EXAMPLE:
$23 \times 34 = 782$ and $24 \times 33 = 792$

a) What happens with other 2 × 2 squares on this grid?

b) What happens if you use a 3 × 3 square instead?

c) What happens with a 2 × 3 rectangle?
Can you predict what might happen before you try?

Q2 Repeat this process with another size grid e.g. 8 × 8 or 12 × 12. Can you spot any patterns?

Q3 Look at these number "walls". Decide on the pattern and then fill in the missing numbers.

a)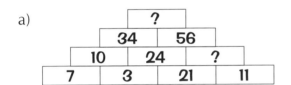

b)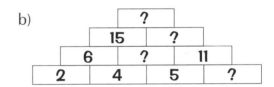

c)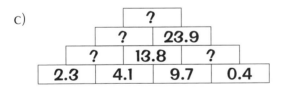

d)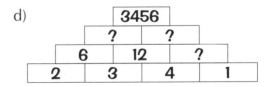

e)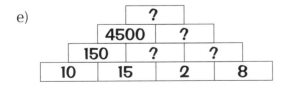

f)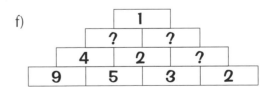

And after all... you're my Numberwall...

Number patterns can be hard to spot — but if you can't see a connection straight away, try adding some numbers together. Or subracting them. Or multiplying/dividing them. Or you could check to see if any numbers are square numbers. Or even/odd numbers. Or prime numbers. Or...

38

Developing Your Problems

Q1 Find the factors of all the numbers from 1 to 20.

    a) List those numbers with only 2 factors. What is the special name of these numbers?

    b) List those with an odd number of factors. What are these numbers called?

    c) Write down the factors of the square numbers up to 100. What do you notice about the number of factors they have?

The factors of a number are all the numbers that divide into it evenly.

Q2 A market is building pig pens like this:

    1 pen — 4 hurdles   2 pens — 7 hurdles   3 pens — 10 hurdles

    a) How many hurdles do they need for 10 pens?

    b) How many hurdles do they need for 50 pens?

    c) Write a rule that calculates how many hurdles are needed for any number of pens.

Q3 The market in the next town builds its pens differently:

    2 pens — 7 hurdles   4 pens (2 x 2) — 12 hurdles   6 pens (2 x 3) — 17 hurdles

    a) How many hurdles do they need for 10 pens?

    b) How many hurdles do they need for 50 pens?

    c) Write a rule that calculates how many hurdles are needed for any number of pens.

Remember the pens are built in pairs.

Q4 Yet another market builds its pens round the perimeter wall.

    a) How many pens can they fit in if each hurdle is 2m long? How many hurdles do they need?

    b) What would happen in a bigger market 50m by 30m?

    c) Investigate other sizes.

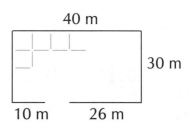

Pig Pen — isn't that a big clock in London...

Questions like this come up quite a lot — doing the <u>first part</u> right helps with the second part and so on, so they're a bit evil. The key is just to <u>practise, practise, practise</u>. Go on — do them again.

Section Three — Solving Problems

Using Algebraic Symbols

Q1   Copy and complete:
The first one is an example for you.

a) $2 + a = 6 \rightarrow a = $ **4**

b) $b + 8 = 12 \rightarrow b = ?$

c) $7 - c = 2 \rightarrow c = ?$

d) $d \times 4 = 20 \rightarrow d = ?$

e) $5e = 30 \rightarrow e = ?$

f) $f \div 2 = 13 \rightarrow f = ?$

g) $g \div 7 = 2 \rightarrow g = ?$

h) $12 \div h = 6 \rightarrow h = ?$

Q2   Simplify these expressions:
e.g. z+z+z+3z = 6z

a) $j + j + j$

b) $2k + 3k$

c) $m + n + m + p + m$

d)   5 lots of q

e) $r \times 6$

f) $5s - 2s$

g) $(t + u) + (t + u)$

h) $5v + 6w - 2v + w$

Q3   Are these mathematical statements true or false?

a) $y \times 3 = 3y$

b) $\dfrac{p}{2x} = \dfrac{p}{x} \times 2$

c) $2x^2 = (2x)^2$

d) $2(n + 3) = 2n + 3$

e) $m^4 = m \times 4$

f)   5 lots of $2n$ = 2 lots of $5n$

Look to see if they work for ALL numbers.

Q4   "Translate" the word equations below into maths equations. Then solve them:

We love maths!

a)   3 lots of x equals 24

b) w divided by 7 = 3

Hint: Give any "unknown" a letter symbol and then write an equation

c)   5 lots of z plus 7 equals 52

d)   A number multiplied by itself equals 36

e)   Think of a number, add 3 and then times by 4 so the answer is 28

f)   Think of a number, divide by 3, then add 3, then times by 3 so the answer is 15

g)   Pocket money – money spent = money saved

h)   Selling price minus buying price = profit

That wasn't the bell — it was an algebraic cymbal...

All those x's and y's and a's and b's aren't really anything special — you can add or multiply letters as if they were normal everyday numbers. And if you collect "like" terms together, you're usually left with an equation that's a bit easier to get to grips with. What more could you want from life...

<u>Algebra Follows Conventions</u>

My life doesn't seem to be following convention...

Q1 Evaluate $\dfrac{(3b-2a)}{4}$ when:

a) $a = 1, b = 2$ e) $a = 9, b = 2$

b) $a = 1, b = 4$ f) $a = 25, b = 10$

c) $a = 10, b = 25$ g) $a = -2, b = 4$

d) $a = 0.2, b = 0.6$ h) $a = -9, b = 2$

Q2 Evaluate $\dfrac{(x^2+y)}{z}$ when: *The answer to this is 3*

a) $x = 2, y = 2, z = 2$ e) $x = 9, y = -6, z = 5$

b) $x = 1, y = 4, z = 10$ f) $x = 4, y = 2, z = -3$

c) $x = 3, y = 6, z = 3$ g) $x = -2, y = 1, z = 0.5$

d) $x = 10, y = 21, z = 11$ h) $x = -3, y = -1, z = -2$

Q3 Which of the expressions below have the same value?

$$ab + c \qquad 12 - (3 + 4) \qquad 12 - (3 - 4) \qquad a(b - c) \qquad a - b - c$$
$$a - (b - c) \qquad a - b + c \qquad c + ba \qquad a - (b + c) \qquad 12 - 3 - 4$$
$$(12 \times 3) + (12 \times 4) \qquad ab - ac \qquad 12 \times (3 + 4) \qquad 12 - 3 + 4$$

Q4 Work out the inverse of each operation below and find the "unknown":

> **EXAMPLE:** $4x - 3 = 5$
>
> So that's "times by four" and then "take away three". → $4x - 3 = 5$
>
> The <u>inverse</u> is "add three" and "divide by four". → $x = (5 + 3) \div 4$ Which means that $\underline{x = 2}$

a) $4m - 8 = 28$ c) $4r + 2 = 2$

b) $n/4 + 3 = 6$ d) $3s - 9 = -3$

"the inverse" sort of means "the opposite".

Simplifying Algebra

Q1 Simplify the expressions below by collecting together "like" terms.

a) $a + a + a + a$

b) $b + b + b + c + c$

c) $d + e + 2f + f + 3d$

d) $4 + 3g - 2 - g$

e) $6h + 4 - 2h - 3 - 4h$

f) $4j + 2j^2 - j + 3j^2$

g) $9 + 2n - 7 - 4n - 2$

h) $24p - 13q - 8p - 4r$

This means putting all the things that are the same together.

Q2 Multiply out these brackets and then simplify.

a) $3(z - 4)$

b) $4(y + 2) - 3(1 - y)$

c) $5(2w - 5) - 2(w + 10)$

d) $6(2v + u) + 2(v + 2u)$

e) $7(t - 2s) - 4(t + 3s)$

f) $3(r + 2s - 3t)$

g) $2(3q - 2p + n) + 4(q + p + n)$

h) $8(m - 2k + 2) + 2(3k - 4)$

Q3 Write expressions for the perimeters of these shapes as simply as possible.

a)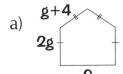

b)

c)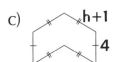

d)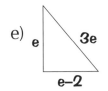

e)

f)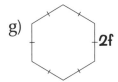

g)

Q4 All these gardens below have a perimeter of 24 m. Calculate the dimensions of each.

a)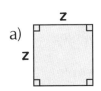

b)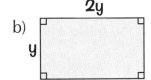

c)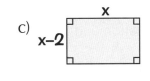

d)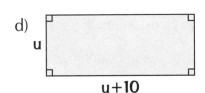

e)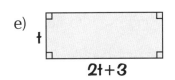

f)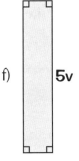

Algebra sends me to sleep quickly — counting n sheep...

Okay, so maybe the word "simplifying" is a bit over-the-top. Algebra will never be *that* simple, but at least you can make things a bit easier for yourself by collecting "like" terms.

Using Linear Equations

Q1   Solve these equations:

a) $j + 7 = 12$ e) $24 = 2p + 14$

b) $2 = 7 - k$ f) $9 = \frac{1}{2}q$

c) $2m + 1 = 23$ g) $12 - \frac{1}{2}r = 10$

d) $4n - 3 = 17$ h) $4.7 + s = 6.1$

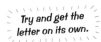

Try and get the letter on its own.

Q2   Simplify these equations and then solve them.

a) $2(x + 1) = 6$ e) $6(x + 1) = 9$

b) $3(3 + x) = 21$ f) $4 = \frac{1}{2}(3x - 4)$

c) $4(2x - 1) = 12$ g) $4x + 3(2x + 4) = 132$

d) $5(2x - 4) = 40$ h) $2(7 - x) + 5x = 23$

Q3   I think of a number, times it by 7, then add 23. The answer is 44.
Write an equation and use it to find my original number.

Q4   Erik is filling cups up with dragon spit from a flask.
He fills 16 × 300 ml cups and has 200 ml of spit left over.

a) Write an equation and use it to find how much spit was in the flask.

Later he fills the flask up with spit, and uses it to fill some 400 ml cups.

b) How many cups will he fill?

c) How much will be left in the bottom of the flask?

Q5   At McDuff's Burger Bar a stack of Little Duff burgers is
1.02m high. Louise Deadcat counts 17 burgers in the stack.

Oh Burger...

a) Write an equation and use it to find the thickness of one burger.

In McDuff's there are three sorts of table, seating 2, 4 or 6 people.
Louise counts 5 full tables of 6, 4 full tables of 4 and 3 people queuing.

b) Write an equation and use it to find how many customers there are.

Later there was 1 table of 2 people, 9 tables of 4, 7 people queuing and a total of 63 customers.

c) Write an equation and use it to find how many tables of 6 there were.

(At McDuff's, all tables have to be full, or they don't let you sit there.)

e-quations — the whole world's going digital...

Linear equations are brilliant for turning really complicated questions into one-liners that you can polish off in a few seconds. They take up less space too, which is also fantastic...

Using Linear Equations

Q1 Substitute values from 1 to 5 for *n* in each of these expressions to produce 8 sequences. Describe each sequence of numbers.

a) *n* + 1	e) *n*/2 + 1
b) 2*n*	f) 3*n* – 3
c) 2*n* + 1	g) 5*n*
d) 3*n*	h) 10 – *n*

Q2 The formula for the area of a triangle is "½ base × height".
Answer these questions, using height = *h*, base = *b*, and area = *A*.

a) If *h* = 4 cm and *b* = 5 cm what is *A*?

b) If *h* = 10 cm and *b* = 6 cm what is *A*?

c) If *b* = 8 m and *A* = 12 m² what is *h*?

d) If *A* = 76 km² and the *h* = 19 km what is *b*?

Q3 Martin's mobile phone has a monthly charge of £15 and a charge of 8p per text message.

a) Convert the monthly charge to pence.

Hint: Call the number of texts n

b) Write a formula to work out how much in pounds Martin has to pay each month.

c) Use your formula to calculate the bill if he sends 20 texts per month.

d) Use your formula to calculate the bill if he sends 120 texts per month.

e) Use your formula to calculate the bill if he sends 15 texts per week.
(Assume a month has 4 weeks.)

Honestly, mobiles are perfectly safe...

Q4 Martin's friend Paul's phone has no monthly charge but costs 50p for each daytime call and 25p for each evening call.

a) Write a formula to calculate Paul's phone bill in pounds.

b) Use the formula to work out his bill if he makes 10 daytime and 30 evening calls.

c) Use the formula to work out his bill if he makes 5 daytime and 100 evening calls.

d) If he made 4 daytime calls and his bill is £25, how many evening calls did he make?

e) If he made 120 evening calls and his bill is £34, how many daytime calls did he make?

You imagined it — you didn't hear the bell...

Linear equations may be as boring as a brown turtleneck jumper, but if you can work out your phone bill with them, they must be useful at least. Just as long as they don't send you to sleep.

Basic Sequences

Q1 For each of these sequences write down and the rule for finding the next number and the next two numbers.

a) 1, 3, 5, 7, ...

b) 297, 299, 301, ...

c) 23, 20, 17, 14, ...

d) 4, 8, 12, 16, ...

e) 12, 19, 26, 33, ...

f) 8, 6, 4, 2, ...

g) 6, 12, 24, 48, ..96..

h) 128, 64, 32, .16.

Q2 Fill in the blanks in these sequences:

a) 13, 16, 19, 22, 25, 28

b) 34, ..., 42, 46, 50, ...

c) 2, 4, 8, 16, 32, 64

d) 16, 8, ..., 2, 1, ...

e) 10, 5, 0, –5, –10, –15

f) 10, 21, 32, 43, 54, 65

g) 63, ..., 45, 36, ..., 18, ..., ...

h) 3, ..., 27, 81, 243

Q3 Below are some number machines. Using 1, 2, 3, 4, 5 as the inputs in each case write down the output from each machine.

> **EXAMPLE:** 4x + 5
>
> 1 → (4 × 1) + 5 = 9
> 2 → (4 × 2) + 5 = 13
> 3 → (4 × 3) + 5 = 17
> 4 → (4 × 4) + 5 = 21
> 5 → (4 × 5) + 5 = 25

a) 2x + 1

b) 3x – 2

c) 5x – 3

d) x + 11

e) 10x – 7

f) 3 – x

g) ½x

h) ½x + 3

Q4 Write down the next two numbers in each sequence:

a) 1, 1, 2, 3, 5, 8, 13 .....

b) 1, 3, 4, 7, 11, 18 .....

c) 1, 5, 6, 11, 17, 28 .....

Sequences — order about all are...

Sequences might seem just like counting in steps, but when everything gets horribly complicated then only Algebra can save the day. See, I told you that Algebra was great. Simply spiffing...

Using Rules of Sequences

Q1 The rules below allow you to work out each term in a sequence from the previous one. Write the first six terms of each.

a) 1st term = 2. Rule: add 3 → 2, 5, 8, 11, 14, 17

b) 1st term = 7. Rule: subtract 1

c) 1st term = 4. Rule: add 7

d) 1st term = 100. Rule: subtract 15

e) 1st term = 4. Rule: times by 3

f) 1st term = 800. Rule: divide by 2

g) 1st term = 3. Rule: times by 10

h) 1st term = 6. Rule: subtract 3

Q2 Use these "nth term" rules to write down the first six terms of these sequences:

a) nth term = $2n$ → 2, 4, 6, 8, 10, 12

b) nth term = $2n + 3$

c) nth term = $2n + 4$

d) nth term = $2n - 1$

e) nth term = $3n$

f) nth term = $3n + 3$

g) nth term = $3n + 4$

h) nth term = $3n - 1$

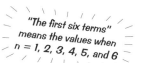
"The first six terms" means the values when $n = 1, 2, 3, 4, 5,$ and 6

A pig in sequins is still a pig

Q3 Write down the 1st, 5th, 10th and 50th terms of sequences generated by these nth terms:

a) $n + 2$

b) $3n$

c) $2n + 1$

d) $n - 2$

e) $10n$

f) $4n - 3$

g) $100 - n$

h) $100 - 2n$

Q4 Work out the first five terms of these sequences. Which pairs of rules generate the same sequence?

a) nth term $4n$

b) 1st term = 2. Rule: add 3 each time

c) nth term = $12 - 2n$

d) 1st term = 20. Rule: add 2 each time

e) 1st term = 10. Rule: subtract 2 each time

f) nth term = $2n + 18$

g) 1st term = 4. Rule: add 4 each time

h) nth term = $3n - 1$

Sequences — what I sew on my frocksies...

Questions on sequences can get pretty tricky alright. It can get a bit jumbled up in your head. So make sure you write everything out — all the stages. That way you don't have to think so hard.

The nth Term

For each sequence of patterns on this page...

a)   Copy and complete the table.

b)   Predict how many lines there will be in the 10th pattern.

c)   Predict how many lines there will be in the 100th pattern.

d)   Write a rule in words to calculate how many sticks are needed for any pattern.

e)   Write the rule in algebra (The nth term = ...).

> **WRITE THE RULE FOR THE NTH TERM**
>
> *That's a rule that'll work for finding the fourth, fifth, sixth, millionth, or... nth number in the sequence.*

Q1

1	2	3	4	5	6

Q2

1	2	3	4	5	6

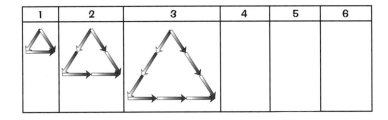

Q3

1	2	3	4	5	6

Q4

1	2	3	4	5	6

Q5   On a piece of cheese each bacterium divides into two every day. If there is one bacterium to start with how many will there be:

a)   after 1 day?   c)   after 3 days?

b)   after 2 days?   d)   after 10 days?

Write a rule in (i) words and (ii) symbols that will allow you to work out how many bacteria there are at any time?

Functions

Q1 Copy and complete these tables showing the inputs and outputs for these functions:

a)

x	2x
1	2
2	4
3	
4	
5	
6	

b)

x	x+1
10	11
11	12
12	
13	
14	
15	

c)

x	2x–3
3	
4	
5	
6	
7	
8	

d)

x	10x
8	
	90
	100
	110
12	
13	

e)

x	12–x
0	
1	
2	
3	
4	
5	

f)

x	0.5x+1
0	
1	
2	
3	
4	
5	

Q2 Write down the expression that creates each of these changes.

That means write down the nth term of the pattern.

a)
1 → 2
2 → 3
3 → 4
4 → 5
5 → 6

b)
0 → 0
1 → 3
2 → 6
3 → 9
4 → 12

c)
10 → 20
11 → 22
12 → 24
13 → 26
14 → 28

d)
10 → 21
11 → 23
12 → 25
13 → 27
14 → 29

EXTRA HINT

Try looking at the gap between the numbers:

3 → 2 (+2)
4 → 4 (+2)
5 → 6 (+2)
6 → 8 (+2)
7 → 10

This gap is two, and it's the same all the way down.

Because it's the same, it means that n is probably being multiplied by a single number... the gap. So try doing n×gap. Then add or subtract to get the right answer.

For this example, it's (n×2)–4. You'd write this as 2n – 4.

Q3 Work out the inverse functions in Q2.

The inverse function does the rule backwards.

It's too early — I have no brain function...

That tip about looking at the gaps is pretty much all you'll need to know to really crack sequences. I guess you might be given something really really tricky, like n^2 or even n^3. You can spot these easily though — the gap will be getting bigger and bigger as you go down the sequence.

Plotting Graphs

Q1 Complete this table for the function $y = x$.
Use the values to plot the line of $y = x$ on the graph.

Plot the graphs for questions 1 to 3 on a single set of axes with values of x between –3 and 3 and y between –6 and 5.

x	–3	–2	–1	0	1	2	3
y				0			3

Q2 Complete this table for the function $y = x + 2$.
Use the values to plot the line of $y = x + 2$ on your graph.

x	–3	–2	–1	0	1	2	3
y	–1			2			

Q3 Complete this table for the function $y = x - 3$.
Use the values to plot the line of $y = x - 3$ on your graph.

x	–3	–2	–1	0	1	2	3
y			–4				0

Q4 Write what you notice about these three graphs.

Q5 Complete this table for the function $y = 2x$.
Use the values to plot the line of $y = 2x$ on your graph.

Do questions 5 to 7 on another graph with values of x between –3 and 3 and y between –9 and 9.

x	–3	–2	–1	0	1	2	3
y		–4			2		6

Q6 Complete this table for the function $y = 3x$.
Use the values to plot the line of $y = 3x$ on your graph.

x	–3	–2	–1	0	1	2	3
y			–3			6	

Q7 Write what you notice about this set of two graphs.

Well that was a graph a minute...

Just like the thoughts of a soap-star, there's nothing complicated about plotting these graphs. But it's dead easy to make silly mistakes — so double-check each point you plot, and you'll be laughing.

Functions and Graphs

Q1   Ali's mobile phone costs him 23p per minute for his phone calls.

   a)   Work out how much he pays for 100 minutes of calls.

   b)   Draw some axes with minutes up to 100 on the x-axis and cost up to £25 on the y-axis.

   c)   Plot a graph of cost against time spent on the phone.

   d)   Use your graph to say how much he pays for 20 minutes of calls.

   e)   Use your graph to say how much he pays for 90 minutes of calls.

   f)   Use your graph to find out how many minutes of calls he can get for £5.75.

   g)   Ali sets himself a spending limit of £15 per month.
         Use your graph to work out how long he can spend on the phone.

Q2   Geri has a different phone tariff. Calls cost 5p
      per minute, and there's a monthly charge of £10.

      *Geri still has to pay the rental,
      even if she makes no calls at all.*

   a)   Copy and complete this table of her costs:

no. of minutes	0	10	20	30	50	100
cost (£)	10					

   b)   Draw some axes with minutes up to 100 along the x-axis and cost up the y-axis.

   c)   Plot a graph of cost against calls made.

   d)   Use your graph to say how much she pays for 40 minutes of calls

   e)   Use your graph to find out how many minutes she can get for £14.00.

   f)   Copy your graph for Q1 on to this graph.

   g)   What can you tell from comparing the two lines?

   h)   Which is the cheaper phone if you want to make 20 minutes of calls per month?

   i)   Which is the cheaper phone if you want to make 90 minutes of calls per month?

Linear Functions and Graphs

Q1   Use the exchange rates in the table on the right to answer the questions below.

STERLING RATES

Currency	Exchange Rate per £1
Australian Dollar	2.8
Danish Kroner	10.5
Turkish Lira	3.1
US Dollar	1.4

a)   How many Danish Kroner would you get in exchange for £10, £20 and £50?

b)   Use your values to plot a line graph with £ on the *x* axis and Danish Kroner on the *y* axis.

c)   Use your graph to find out how many Danish Kroner you'd get for £35.

d)   If you needed 250 Danish Kroner how many £ would you have to pay?

Q2   Repeat Q1 but using US dollars instead.

Q3   The table below shows the temperatures at midday in London for 10 days in March. Plot the temperatures on a graph with the date on the *x*-axis and temperature on the *y*-axis.

Day in March	4th	5th	6th	7th	8th	9th	10th	11th	12th	13th
Temp. (°C)	8	10	11	4	2	1	7	15	14	9

a)   Join the points up with straight lines.

b)   Why can't you use the graph to say what the temperature was at midnight on April 3rd?

Q4   Match the graphs below to a suitable function chosen from a) to f).

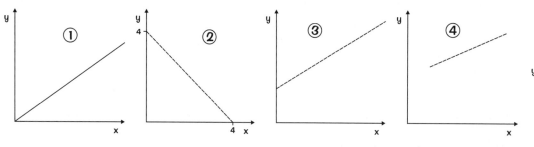

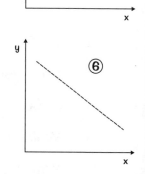

a)   Heating bill against average outside temperature.

b)   Cost of a mobile phone on a monthly contract against number of calls made.

c)   Money left in the bank against money spent.

d)   Temperature against hours of sunshine.

e)   Ideal weight against height for 12 year old boys.

f)   Money spent against number of "Mercury Bars" bought.

Basic Geometry

Q1   Use this diagram to complete the following:

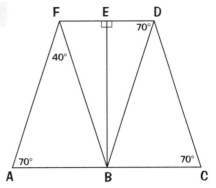

a)   AB is _____ to ED

b)   EB is _____ to AC

c)   FB is parallel to _____

d)   FD is perpendicular to _____

e)   FDB is an _____

f)   EDB is a _____

g)   FDBA is a _____

h)   ACDF is a _____

i) $F\hat{A}B$ = ____°

j) $B\hat{C}D$ = ____°

k) $B\hat{D}E$ = ____°

l)   AB = ____ = _____

m)   AF = ___ = ____ = ____

Q2   Name these polygons:

a)

b)

c)

POLLY!

Where's Polly Gone?

d)

e)

f)

g)

Flew to the jungle all alone at dawn,
Back into the nest where I was born,
The monkeys in the tree didn't say "hello" to meeee....

Wednesday Night Karaoke Extravaganza

h)

i)

j)

k)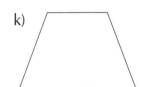

If I hear one more parrot joke..

Learn the names and number of sides of all the shapes. Polygons' names end in "-gon" and begin with a bit that tells us the number of sides, e.g "pent-" for five, "oct-" for eight etc... If all the sides are the same length then they are called "regular" polygons — easy as that.

Angles and Triangles

Q1 What angles do the letters represent?

a)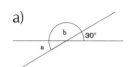

b)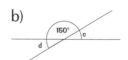

c)

d)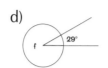

e)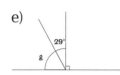

f)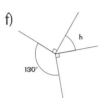

g)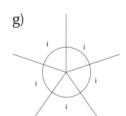

h)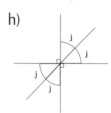

Waah! MUM, That's NOT FAIR!! Sarah got 28° of cake and I only got 26°!

The sum of the interior (inside) angles of a triangle add up to 180°

Degrees round a point add up to 360°

Q2 Find the missing angles in these triangles:

a)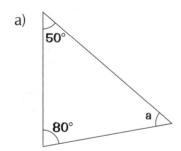
50°
80°
a

b)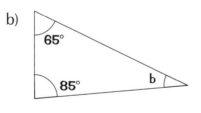
65°
85°
b

c)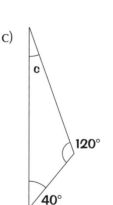
c
120°
40°

d)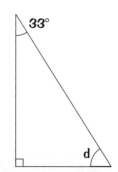
33°
d

e)
26°
e   e

f)
f
f   48°

Sides marked with the *lines* are the *same length*

Where can you buy angles — at a corner shop... (hahaha)

If you remember that the angles in a triangle or along a straight line add up to 180°, then you can't go far wrong with this topic really. So just remember those facts and the whole topic will be a piece of cake. Cake, hmmm... the angles in a round cake add up to 360°. Remember that too...

Sketching 2D Shapes

Q1   Copy and label these triangles as either equilateral, isosceles, scalene or right-angled.

a)   b)    c)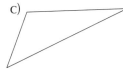

d) 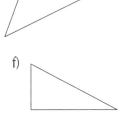   e)   f)

Q2   Copy and label these quadrilaterals as either square, rectangle, rhombus, parallelogram, trapezium, kite, irregular and concave or irregular and convex.

a)    b)   c) 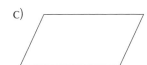   d)

e)    f) 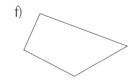   g) 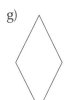   h)

Q3   a)   Draw a square 20 cm × 20 cm.

b)   Draw a line to join the mid-point of each side to the two nearest midpoints, forming a second square.

c)   What fraction is the new square of the original one?

d)   You have also formed 4 triangles. What fraction of the original square is 1 triangle?

e)   Draw a third square inside the second one. Work out the fractions again.

Q4   What are the angles in an equilateral triangle?

a)   Draw and cut out 6 identical equilateral triangles.

b)   Put them together to form a regular hexagon.

c)   What does this tell you about the angles in a regular hexagon?

2D, or not 2D — that is the question...

Enjoy this while it lasts, my friend — it's not every maths lesson that you get marks for drawing things and cutting shapes out. There are a few names to remember, like types of triangles, but it could be worse, usually you have to do questions about algebra and all sorts of other nasty stuff.

Basics of Using Polygons

Q1   Here is a sequence of shapes. Answer the questions below without drawing anything else:

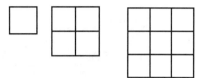

Size of Square	1×1	2×2	3×3	4×4
Number of 1×1 squares	1	4	9	16
Number of 2×2 squares	0	1	4	
Number of 3×3 squares	0	0		
Number of 4×4 squares	0	0		
Total number of squares	1	5		

a)   Complete the table.

b)   Can you spot any patterns?

c)   What may happen for a 5×5 square?

d)   Draw a 5×5 square and test your predictions.

Q2   Draw a regular hexagon, label its vertices from A to F and label its centre X.
Join up opposite vertices through the centre X. Find the following shapes:

a)   A trapezium.

b)   A rhombus.

c)   An equilateral triangle.

d)   A concave heptagon.

e)   A concave hexagon.

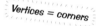
Vertices = corners

I'm just a regular kind of guy...

Q3   Use the fact that angles in any triangle add up to 180° to calculate all the angles in this shape.

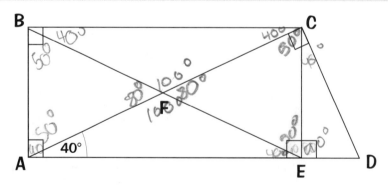

a)   Draw 3 different quadrilaterals from the diagram above.
Name them and find the sum of their (internal) angles.

b)   Notice anything?

Have you heard the one about the parrot... — Aarrgh...

There are loads of odd names here, which is a shame. It'd be so much easier if we could all use sensible names like sixagon or sevenagon. But someone, somewhere decided that we all need to learn weirdy-sounding names like hexagon and heptagon. If I ruled the world, it'd all be so different.

Using Polygons (some trickier stuff)

Q1   Fill in all the missing angles in this shape.

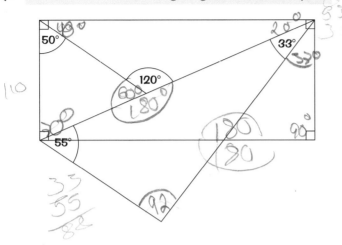

Q2   Find all the angles marked in these regular polygons:

a) 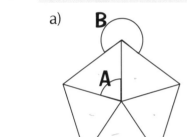   b) 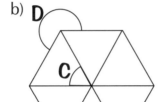   c) 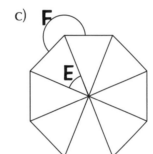   d)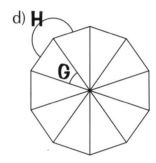

Q3   Make a copy of this diagram and label all the angles at the vertices correctly.

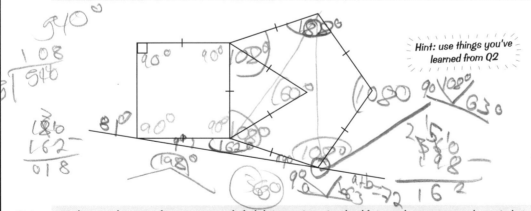

Hint: use things you've learned from Q2

Fold what which way?

Q4   Take a sheet of paper and fold it twice in half (as shown on the right).
Imagine you are going to cut off the corner of your new shape
(the corner that was in the middle of the paper before you folded it).

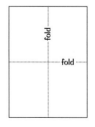

a)   What shape hole do you think you will make?

b)   Cut it and see.

I can't do these any more — I'm a polygoner...

It's one of those pages where you don't need to know that much to be able to do the questions —
but you have to keep using the same fact over and over again. It might get a bit boring, but it
means you won't forget how to do this kind of question in a hurry. Which is a very good thing.

3D Shapes

Q1 Draw nets of the following solids:

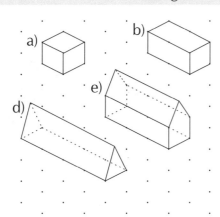 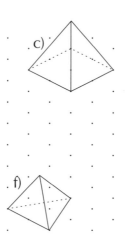 

Q2 From these nets pick two that will make a cube and 2 that will make an open-topped cube.

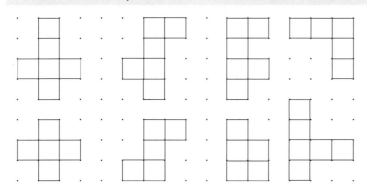

Q3 Draw a plan (looking down) and two elevations (looking from the side) of these 3D solids.

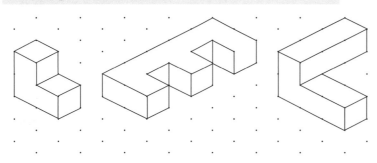 

Q4 Use isometric/dotty paper to draw the solids that can be made from these nets:

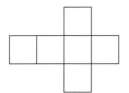 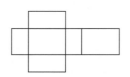 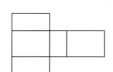

All these nets — they're driving me dotty...

It can be a bit tricky to do paper folding in your head, which is what all this amounts to. But let's face it, it's better than questions with x and y in. So enjoy the fun while it lasts I say.

Reflection

Q1   Trace these diagrams and then reflect each shape in the mirror line, M.

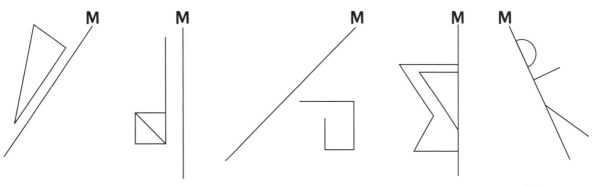

Q2   Trace these diagrams showing shapes and their reflections. Draw each mirror line and label it m.

Q3   Copy the diagram on the right and label the rectangle R.

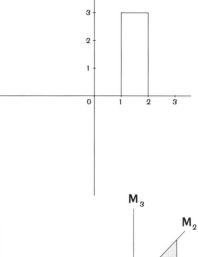

a)   Reflect the rectangle R in the *x* axis to make a new image S.

b)   Reflect S in the *y* axis to form a second image T.

c)   Reflect T in the *x* axis to form a third image U.

d)   How could you reflect U back on to R?

Q4   Form the image of this triangle across the mirror line M_1.
Then mirror the whole pattern you have made in M_2.
Do the same in M_3 to complete the pattern.
(Remember each time to mirror the **whole image**).
How many lines of symmetry has your shape?

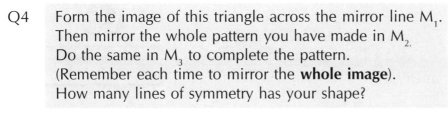

Reflection — there's another world out there...

Reflection is about how things look back to front. Mirror lines show where you would place a mirror in order to see a reflection. Try putting a mirror on the lines drawn in the above questions. Do you get the same shapes? Put the mirror in different positions and see how the reflection changes.

Rotation

Q1   Copy this graph.

a)   Rotate shape A through 90° clockwise with centre (0,0) to form the image B.

b)   Rotate shape A through 180° with centre (0,0) to form the image C.

c)   Rotate shape A through 180° with centre (2,2) to form the image D.

d)   Rotate shape C through 90° anticlockwise with centre (-4,-2) to form the image E.

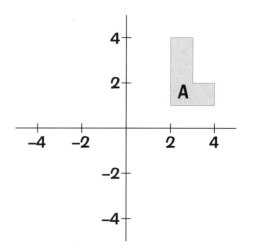

Q2   Draw a set of axes with x and y from −5 to 5.

a)   Plot the points A (1,1)   B (1,3)   C (3,3)   D (3,1) and join to form a square.

b)   Rotate ABCD 90° clockwise with centre (0,0) to form $A_1B_1C_1D_1$.

c)   Rotate ABCD 90° anticlockwise with centre (0,0) to form $A_2B_2C_2D_2$.

d)   Rotate ABCD 180° clockwise with centre (3,3) to form $A_3B_3C_3D_3$.

e)   Rotate ABCD 90° clockwise with centre (3,1) to form $A_4B_4C_4D_4$.

Q3   On another graph with x and y from 0 to 5 draw the square ABCD from Q2. Using (2,2) as the centre of rotation:

a)   Rotate through 90° clockwise.

b)   Rotate through 180°.

c)   Rotate through 270° clockwise.

d)   What do you notice?

Too much rotation can be a bad thing.

Q4   Draw two examples of:

a)   A figure with 4 lines of symmetry.

b)   A figure with rotational symmetry order 3.

c)   A figure with rotational symmetry order 4 but no lines of symmetry.

Round, round, gettaround, I gettaround...

If you're snowboarding down a huge half-pipe trying to pull off some mean backside 360 experimental you're gonna need to know about rotation (which is a type of "transformation").

Translation and other Transformations

Q1 Copy this diagram and then draw the image of the shaded triangle after each translation.

a) 4 units to the right — label the triangle A.

b) 2 units up — label the triangle B.

c) 3 units right then 2 units down — label triangle C.

d) 2 units left, then 1 unit up — label triangle D.

e) What translation moves triangle D back onto the shaded triangle?

f) What translation moves triangle C onto the triangle A?

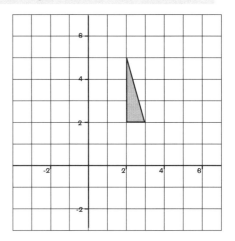

Q2 Use this diagram to describe the following translations:

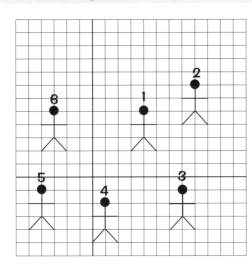

a) Person 1 on to person 2.

b) Person 1 on to person 3.

c) Person 1 on to person 4.

d) Person 1 on to person 5.

e) Person 1 on to person 6.

f) Person 3 on to person 5.

g) Person 5 on to person 3.

h) Person 3 on to person 6.

Remember that "transformations" include rotation, reflection AND translation!

Q3 Describe the following transformations:

a) B to D f) E to F

b) B to A g) G to B

c) B to F h) H to G

d) F to C i) C to B

e) E to B j) B to C

If you can't work out the equation of a mirror line then just give 2 points on the line.

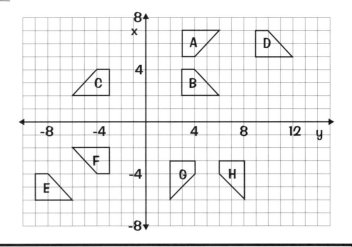

Translation — not just something for French class...

Translation means that an object is moved relative to its starting position. It's as if you're sliding the shape across the graph paper. So a translation of (2,4) would be sliding the shape two across, and then four up. And that's it — translation is definitely the easiest transformation to work out.

Coordinates

Q1 Draw axes from –6 to 6 on both x and y axes. Then plot the following points and join them up (in order) to make letters. What word do they spell?

   a)   (-5,1) (-4,1) (-4,3) (-2,3) (-2,4) (-4,4) (-4,5) (-2,5) (-2,6) (-5,6), (-5,1)

   b)   (1,1) (4,1) (4,2) (3,2) (3,5) (4,5) (4,6) (1,6) (1,5) (2,5) (2,2) (1,2) (1,1)

   c)   (-2,0) (-5,0) (-5,-3) (-3,-3) (-3,-4) (-5,-4) (-5,-5) (-2,-5) (-2,-2) (-4,-2) (-4,-1) (-2,-1), (-2,0)

   d)   (1,0) (2,0) (2,-2) (3,-2) (3,0) (4,0) (4,-5) (3,-5) (3,-3) (2,-3) (2,-5) (1,-5), (1,0)

Q2 Find the missing points in the shapes below. The answer to part a) is on the right.

   a)   A square with coordinates (2,2) (2,4) (4,2)

   b)   A square with coordinates (1,2) (2,2) (2,1)

   c)   A rectangle with coordinates (0,0) (5,2) (0,2)

   d)   A rectangle with coordinates (-3,2) (1,2) (1,-3)

   e)   A rhombus with coordinates (7,5) (10,3) (13,5)

   f)   A kite with coordinates (6,2) (8,6) (6,8)

   g)   A rhombus with coordinates (-3,4) (-6,8) (-3,12)

   h)   A parallelogram with coordinates (2,0) (0,-4) (6,-4)

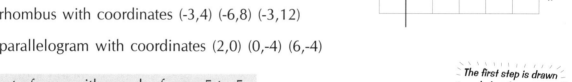

Q3 Draw a set of axes with x and y from –5 to 5.

   Starting at the origin (0,0) follow this sequence:

   1 Add 1 to the x coordinate — write down the new coordinates and plot the new point.

   2 Add 1 to the y coordinate — write down the new coordinates and plot the new point.

   3 Take 2 from the x coordinate — write down the new coordinates and plot the new point.

   4 Take 2 from the y coordinate — write down the new coordinates and plot the new point.

The first step is drawn below for you.

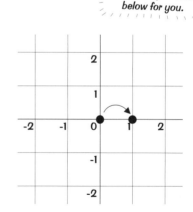

Experiment with similar sequences to draw different patterns.

   5 Add 3 to the x coordinate — write down the new coordinates and plot the new point.

   6 Add 3 to the y coordinate — write down the new coordinates and plot the new point.

   7 Continue until you are clear what the pattern will look like. Describe the pattern.

I can't do these — I'm too uncoordinated...

Plotting a coordinate isn't too hard. It's when you've got to do a load that it gets tricky — go too fast and you're bound to make a mistake or two. Best take it slow, and double-check each point.

Constructing Shapes

Q1   Measure these lines to the nearest millimetre.

a) _____

b) _____

c) _____

d) _____

e) _____

f) _____

g) ___

h) _____

Q2   Measure these angles to the nearest degree.

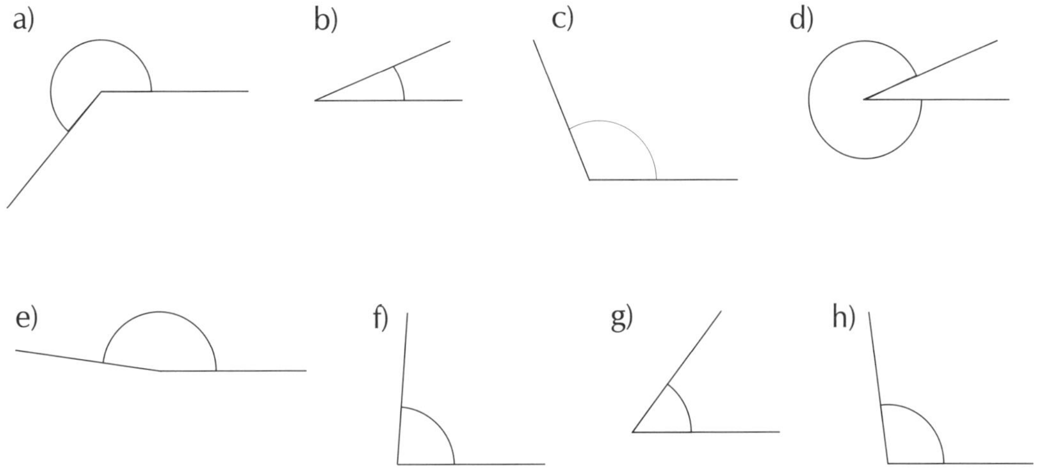

a)   b)   c)   d)

e)   f)   g)   h)

Q3   Use a ruler and a protractor to draw the following shapes:

a)   A triangle of side length and enclosed angle of:

     i)   5cm, 5cm and 30° 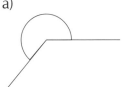   iii)   6cm, 8 cm and 100°

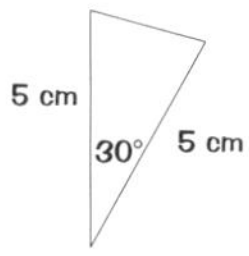

     ii)   3 cm, 6 cm and 45°   iv)   5cm, 8 cm and 90°

b)   A triangle with two angles and enclosed side length of:

     i)   40°, 90°, enclosed side 6.5 cm   ii)   40°, 60°, enclosed side 8 cm

c)   A rhombus with one angle and equal sides of:

     i)   40° and 4cm   ii)   120° and 5cm

Q4   Use a ruler and compasses to construct an accurate net for each of these shapes:

a)   Square based pyramid — base 4cm by 4cm; slope edge 5cm.

b)   Square based pyramid — base 4cm by 4cm; slope edge 8cm.

c)   Equilateral triangular prism — triangle sides 3cm; length 7 cm.

d)   Isosceles triangular prism — triangle 2 cm, 4cm, 4cm; length 6 cm.

e)   Regular tetrahedron — edges 5 cm.

Imperial and Metric Units

Q1   Copy and complete:

a) 3.0 m = ... cm = ... mm

d) ..... m = ... cm = 1000 mm

g) 5.7 km = ... m

b) 2.5 m = ... cm = ... mm

e) ..... m = ... cm = 5500 mm

h) ..... km = 4400 m

c) ..... m = 500 cm = ... mm

f) 0.5 m = ... cm = ... mm

1000 kg = 1 tonne

Q2   Copy and complete:

a) 1 litre = ... cl = ... ml

d) ..... litre = ... cl = 500 ml

g) ..... g = ... kg = 1 tonne

b) 2 litre = ... cl = ... ml

e) 2000 g = ... kg

h) 9300 kg = ... tonnes

c) ..... litre = 350 cl = ... ml

f) ..... g = 7.4 kg

Q3   Sketch a square 0.1m by 0.1m. How many cm² can you fit inside? How many cm² could you fit inside a square 1m by 1m? Sketch a square 1cm by 1cm (1 cm²). How many mm² can you fit inside? Use these answers to help you complete the following:

a) 1 m^2 = ... cm^2

c) 1 cm^2 = ... mm^2

e) 10 m^2 = ... cm^2

b) 1.5 m^2 = ... cm^2

d) ..... cm^2 = 300 mm^2

f) 1 m^2 = ... cm^2 = ... mm^2

Q4   Read the following scales:

a)   b)   c)   d)   e)   f)

g)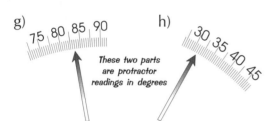

75 80 85 90   h) 30 35 40 45

These two parts are protractor readings in degrees

i) **1:14:52.7**   j) **0:47:26.1**

These two parts are stop-watch readings in hours, minutes, seconds and tenths of a second.

Q5   Lucy and her Grandad are a bit weird — they're comparing units.

Join them in their weirdness and convert all of Lucy's list of quantities into imperial units and all of Grandad's list into metric units. Use the conversion chart to help you.

Conversions

8 pints = 1 gall = approx. 5 litres
5 miles = approx. 8 km
1 kg = approx. 2.2 lb
1 in = approx. 2.5 cm
1 lb = 16 oz = approx. 450 g
0.9m = approx. 1 yd = 36 inches

Lucy's List

Distance from Lancaster to Preston - 41 km
Pet Cat weighs 3.4 kg
Thermos flask holds 0.75 litres
Jar of chilli holds 125 g
Bedroom door is 1.9 m tall

Grandad's List

Manchester to Edinburgh - 224 miles
6 gallons of petrol costs £23.80
Garden canes are 82 inches long
Haggis 6 lb

Measuring Angles

Q1 Are these angles acute, right-angled, obtuse or reflex?

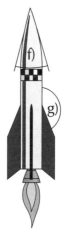
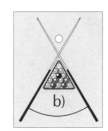

Q2 Estimate the size of these angles.

a)   b)   c)   d)

e)   f) 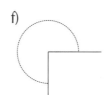   g)   h)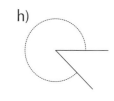

Q3 Fred is facing North. How many degrees does he turn through if he:

a) Turns clockwise to face E?   d) Turns clockwise to face W?

b) Turns anticlockwise to face S?   e) Turns clockwise to face SE?

c) Turns anticlockwise to face E?   f) Turns anticlockwise to face NW?

Q4 Sanjeet is facing East. How many degrees does she turn through if she turns:

a) Clockwise to face S?   c) Anticlockwise to face N?   e) Clockwise to face SE?

b) Anticlockwise to face S?   d) Clockwise to face W?   f) Anticlockwise to face NW?

Q5 On the tombola stall at the Stonehedge Fête the arrow points to the prize you have won. The arrow always starts from X. Which prize does Harold win if the arrow spins:

a) Anticlockwise through 315°?   d) Anticlockwise through 675°?

b) Clockwise through 225°?   e) Clockwise through 810°?

c) Clockwise through 900°?   f) Anticlockwise through 450°?

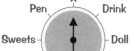

A four-legged animal, not often eaten by humans.

Area and Perimeter

Q1 Find the perimeter and the area of these rectangles, and the area of each shaded triangle.

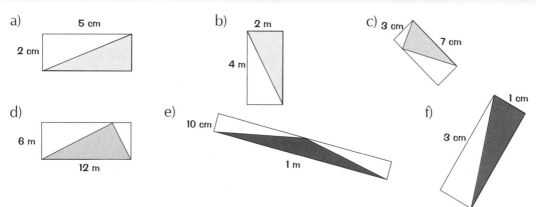

a)
5 cm
2 cm

b)
2 m
4 m

c)
3 cm
7 cm

d)
6 m
12 m

e)
10 cm
1 m

f)
1 cm
3 cm

Q2 Find the area and perimeter of these shapes.

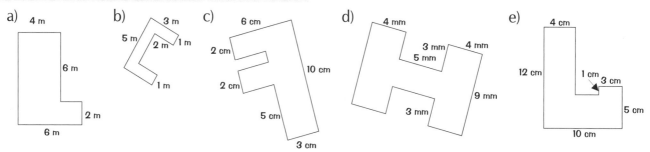

a)
4 m
6 m
2 m
6 m

b)
3 m
5 m
2 m
1 m
1 m

c)
6 cm
2 cm
2 cm
10 cm
5 cm
3 cm

d)
4 mm
3 mm
5 mm
4 mm
9 mm
3 mm

e)
4 cm
12 cm
1 cm
3 cm
5 cm
10 cm

Q3 All these shapes have the same area. Fill in the missing dimensions.

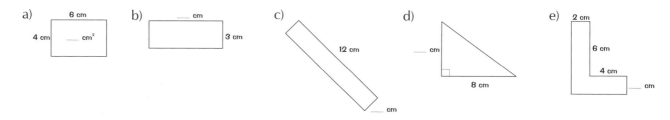

a)
6 cm
4 cm
___ cm²

b)
___ cm
3 cm

c)
12 cm
___ cm

d)
___ cm
8 cm

e)
2 cm
6 cm
4 cm
___ cm

Q4 Sketch 5 shapes with different areas which all have a perimeter of 16 cm.

Q5 Sketch 5 shapes with different perimeters which all have an area of 16 cm².

Q6 Sketch these shapes.

a) A rectangle with area 18 m² and perimeter 22 m.

b) A rectangle with area 30 cm² and perimeter 22 cm.

c) A square with perimeter 28 cm. What is its area?

d) A triangle with area 14 m² and base 7 m.

I love you, Mr. Fish

She's a babe.

This is no sweat for me now — I'm area-conditioned...

This stuff on areas and perimeters is probably some of the easiest stuff in your Key Stage 3 Maths. For perimeters, count each side round from a point until you get back to that point. And as for areas of rectangles... they're even easier — times the width by the height. That's it.

Area and Volume

Q1 Have a look at the diagram on the right.

a) How many 1 cm³ cubes fit inside this cuboid?

b) How many faces has the cuboid got?

c) Work out the area of each face.

d) Work out the total surface area of the cuboid

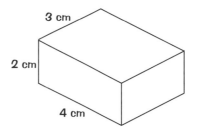

Sketch the net of each one... if you want — it might help.

Q2 Below are some cubes and cuboids.

a) Work out the volumes of these cubes and cuboids.

b) Calculate the surface area of each one.

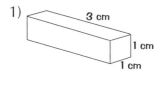
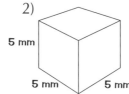
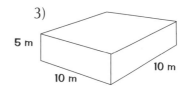

Q3 Find the volumes of these triangular prisms: *Hint: they are half of a cuboid*

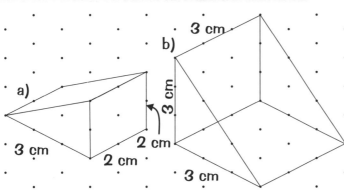
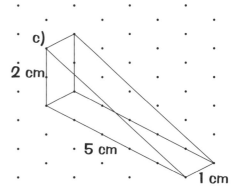

Q4 Wow-These-Taste-Fantastic Sweets are about to launch a new product "Bubblegum Boxes". Each piece of bubble gum is a cube with sides 1 cm.

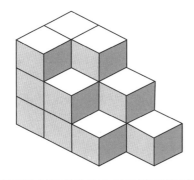

a) If the company wants to sell them packed in 12s, what different packing arrangements are there?

b) Which one uses least wrapping paper?

c) There are to be 24 pieces in the jumbo pack, what arrangements can there be?

d) Which jumbo pack uses least wrapping paper?

Pass me the bag — I'm suffering from area-sickness...

You have to find ways to make tricky questions simpler. The triangular prisms above were half of a cuboid. And volumes of cuboids are easy. So you've made triangular prisms easy too. Great.

Collecting Data

Q1 The governors of a school are worried about traffic safety immediately outside the school and are planning a survey.

a) Make a list of things that they could investigate.

b) Choose a good time to carry out the survey and say why you have chosen this time.

c) A woman who lives next door to the school offers to count cars outside the school gates after she gets home from work. Why is this not likely to be very helpful?

Q2 The headteacher is concerned about the traffic caused by parents dropping off and collecting pupils at the school gate.

a) Make a list of things that you think could influence how parents get their children to school.

b) Use your list to think of some questions that the headteacher could ask parents.

Q3 Clarissa is trying to choose a book as a present for her younger brother who is 6 years old.

a) Make a list of ways she could decide if a book was suitable.

b) Use this list to compare a children's book with an adult book. Would your list really have been useful?

Q4 Take two different (but equally fantastic) CGP books and answer the following questions. (I guess you could use other books... though they wouldn't be as amazingly fantastic...)

a) How much of each page is picture and how much is words? (Estimate the area of the pictures and the area of words).

b) Choose a paragraph from each book and compare the number of words in each sentence.

c) Compare the lengths of the words used in each book. (You could use averages...)

My birthday — it's a data remember...

This lot's all pretty simple if you use some common sense. Which makes a change from all the rest of the stuff you've had to do. Most of that is learning a method, and learning it good.

Selecting Data

Q1 Shaznay is looking at what schoolchildren buy in their school canteen.

a) She wants to be sure she has a good cross-section.
How should she choose a suitable sample of pupils?

b) Should she repeat her survey on another day?
How can she be sure the data is not biased?

Q2 Melanie is investigating buying patterns at McDuff's burger restaurant — she's going to survey customers in the shop.

a) What should she ask?

b) Is it necessary to ask every customer?

c) She can only visit the restaurant for one hour after school.
Will she get a good sample? If not, why?

Q3 The Weirdy Broadcasting Company are about to launch a new TV channel and they want to find out which programmes people like best. For each of the sampling methods below, say whether you think it is good or bad. Explain your answers.

a) Survey people chosen at random from the phone directory and who answer the phone between 10 am and 12 pm on a Tuesday.

b) Survey all the children leaving school one afternoon.

c) Survey people shopping in a large market town over one week.

d) Survey people visiting "Ladies' Day" at the Ascot Races.

e) Survey a random selection of people from the electoral roll.

f) Survey people from the front of the London telephone directory.

g) Survey people who've landed on the moon since 1969.

Which one would you choose? Give reasons for your choice.

Q4 The government is planning its spending on Education for the next 20 years.
Where could they look for the data they need about numbers, gender and location?

Collecting Data

Q1   Design a suitable tally chart to collect data about the number and type
      of vehicles for a traffic survey. Use time periods of 15 minutes.

Q2   Design suitable questions with "tick boxes" to collect the following information:

   a)   How children get to school.

   b)   How long their journey time is.

   c)   Whether they come on their own or with others.

   d)   Whether or not they use public transport (if it is available).

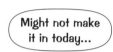

Might not make
it in today...

Q3   Design a tally chart to measure the lengths of sentences on a page
      of a book. Group the sentences into 1-5 words, 6-10 words etc.

School
Elephant

Q4   You are going to collect data from a train station about
      how long people take to travel to and from work each day.

   a)   Decide on suitable class intervals for the journey time.

   b)   Design a question and a tally chart that you could easily use.

Q5   Class 7P are designing surveys to use in the school. An example is
      given below. Can you spot any problems? Could you improve them?

1. How far do you travel to school?

1 mile	2 miles	3 miles	4 miles	5 miles

2. What is your favourite food? _____

3. How many children are in your maths class?

1-15	15-20	20-25	25-30

4. How much television do you watch?

0-1 hrs	1-2 hrs	2-3 hrs	3-4 hrs	4-5 hrs

Practise this stuff on a data-day basis...

Collecting data's a pretty okay topic compared to some you get in maths. Just keep all your
questions simple, and make sure that the possible answers are useful — so don't write a question
to ask how old someone is and have tick boxes for 0-100, 100-200 etc. That's just silly.

Mean, Mode, Median and Range

Q1 Find the mode of the following sets of numbers.

a) 2, 6, 3, 8, 1, 4, 5, 8, 5, 2, 5, 3, 7, 3, 8, 7, 8, 1

b) 25, 21, 25, 21, 23, 21, 23, 29

c) 0.4, 0.3, 0.2, 0.4, 0.1, 0.2, 0.3, 0.4

d) 10, 7, 8, 10, 7, 8, 9, 7, 10

e) 107, 106, 103, 108, 104, 106, 105, 105, 106

Q2 Work out the median and range of each of these sets of numbers.

a) 4, 3, 8, 5, 7, 6, 3, 6, 8   d) 12, 17, 14, 9, 19, 14

b) 5, 6, 3, 9, 10, 13, 3   e) 91, 98, 95, 92, 96, 93

c) 0.3, 0.2, 0.1, 0.4, 0.7, 0.34, 0.45   f) 38, 45, 39, 32, 40, 32

Q3 Calculate the mean of each of these sets of data.

a) 3, 4, 6, 8, 9   c) 101, 102, 104, 105, 105, 113

b) 24, 25, 26, 26, 30, 31   d) 1.1, 1.3, 1.4, 1.8, 2.1, 2.3, 2.4

Q4 Larks and Spenders are analysing their sales. Find the median and mode of:

a) Dress sizes: 18, 10, 12, 12, 16, 12, 16, 16, 14, 10,
                     14, 14, 14, 14, 16, 12, 14, 16, 14, 18

b) Shoes:

4	$4\frac{1}{2}$	5	$5\frac{1}{2}$	6	$6\frac{1}{2}$
||||	||||	卌 ||	卌 |||	卌 ||	卌

c) Babygrows: 6 months (6),   9 months (3),   18 months (1).

d) Chocolate bars: 3 × 50g, 5 × 100 g, 6 × 150g

More chocolate!
I want MORE!

Uh-oh... He's
going to blow.

Mean, Mode, Median and Range

Q1   The mean weight of 4 boys is 53 kg and the mean weight of 3 girls is 48 kg. Work out:

    a)   The total weight of the boys.

    b)   The total weight of the girls.

    c)   The weight of all 7 children together.

    d)   The mean weight of all the children. Give your answer to 1 d.p.

Q2   The mean weight of 3 boys is 56 kg and the mean weight of 4 girls is 51 kg. Work out the mean of all seven children.

Use the method from Q1

Q3   The mean of 5 numbers is 8. The median is 9, the mode is 5 and the range is 6. Can you find the numbers?

Q4   The mean of 5 numbers is 14, the mode is 15, the median is 15, the range is 5 and the largest number is 16. What are the numbers?

Q5   The Stonetown basketball team scored a mean of 21 points per game last season when they played 10 matches. In the first 9 matches they scored 6, 23, 30, 20, 7, 46, 12, 13, and 24. What did they score in the last match?

Q6   For each of these sets of data work out the (i) mean, (ii) median, (iii) mode, and (iv) range.

    a)   Men's Shirt Sizes

14	14	15	15½	15½
15½	15½	16	16	16½

    b)   Maths Test Results   1   13   14   20   21   23   23   25   26   27   30

    c)   Hourly Wage Rates

£3.20	£3.25	£3.65	£4.20	£4.35	£4.90
£5.60	£5.60	£6.10	£6.10	£15.50	

    d)   Children's Ages   1   1   1   7   8   9   9   10   15   16   17

    e)   Values of cars sold in a week

£5600	£5600	£7800	£9000	£10 000
£10,500	£12,000	£15,000	£33,000	£56,000

    f)   Lottery wins in one town   £10 £10 £10 £10 £10 £10 £10 £10 £60 £25,000

    g)   More test results   1   2   2   3   4   35   36   36   37   37

Constructing Graphs and Charts

Q1 Copy and complete this table and draw a pie chart to show the information.

Favourite TV Soap	Number of Viewers	Degrees
Riverside	15	30°
Westenders	45	
Far and Away	30	
Grimdale	30	
Abdication Street	60	
TOTAL		

Q2 Draw a pie chart to show the following information about David's farm.

Animal	Cattle	Sheep	Pig	Chicken	Ostrich
Number	60	180	40	70	10

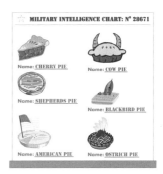

Q3 Draw a line bar graph showing how David's farm is divided.

CROP	Grass	Barley	Oats	Linseed	Rape Seed Oil
ACRES	90	30	30	10	20

Q4 Here are the results of a survey taken in 2 classes at Patsy's school.

a) Draw a dual bar graph to show this information.

b) Describe the differences you can see.

No of cars per family	Class A Frequency	Class B Frequency
0	3	1
1	15	10
2	9	13
3	2	5
4 or more	1	1

I worked hard at this page — I'm a grafter...

Graphs and charts are dead useful, although they get a bit 'samey' when you've done a few. But it's better to do quite a lot and get really good at them, because you're less likely to forget how to do them later. Which I would say is a good thing, all things considered.

Understanding Graphs and Charts

Q1 This pie chart shows the proportions of votes for candidates in the local election.

a) Measure and write down the angles in the pie chart.

b) What fraction of people voted for Sally?

c) If 180 people voted for Sally, how many voted in total?

d) How many voted for Diana?

e) Who got the least votes?

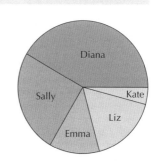

Q2 These pie charts below show some stuff about the pies that Jimmy and James have been eating. Jimmy has eaten 500 pies; James has eaten 100 pies.

a) James reckons he has eaten more cheese and onion pies than Jimmy. Explain why he is wrong.

b) Jimmy hates turkey and cranberry pies — though he still ate a fair few. How many did he eat?

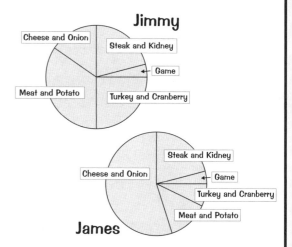

Q3 This diagram shows how a local council spent its budget.

a) What fraction of the budget was spent on education?

b) What fraction of the budget was spent on fire and rescue?

c) Calculate how many degrees represent roads and transport.

d) The total budget was £300m. How much was spent on each category?

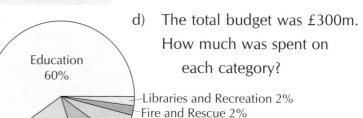

Q4 This bar chart shows the number of members for five different clubs at a school.

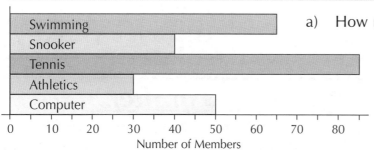

a) How many people belong to the athletics club?

b) Which is the most popular club?

c) How many more people belong to the swimming club than the computer club?

Comparing Distributions

Q1   Here are some statistics about the number of words per sentence in 2 books:
Book A — mean 12.5, range 30.   Book B — mean 8.2, range 12.

   a)   Which book do you think might be more suitable for children learning to read?

   b)   Can you be sure? What other information might you need?

Q2   Here is a bar graph showing pet ownership in year 7 of 2 different schools:

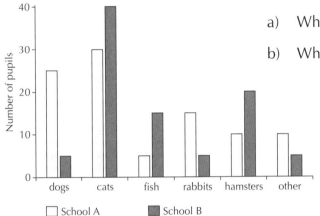

   a)   Which school's pupils have more pets in total?

   b)   Which school has more cats?

   c)   How many more rabbits do the pupils of school A have than those of school B?

Q3   Appleton has a population whose ages have median 34, mean 29 and range 90.
Orangeburgh has a population whose ages have median 45, mean 36 and range 98.

   a)   Predict which town has the highest proportion of young families and children.

   b)   Which town do you think has the older population?

Q4   The pie charts below show the amount of post
delivered to two different companies over a week:

Bodgit Ltd.

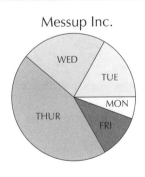
Messup Inc.

   a)   Which day does Bodgit Ltd. have most post?

   b)   Which day does Messup Inc. have most post?

   c)   Which company has a higher proportion of its post on Fridays?

No more pies please — I'm stuffed...

Noticed how you always get hungry when you start doing questions on pie charts? I've just
nobbled one of those massive bars of chocolate — you know, the really huge ones. That's why I
can't think of much useful to tell you — I feel far too ill. I'll do better next time... I promise...

Probability Using Words

Q1 Match one of these words to each statement: CERTAIN, LIKELY, UNLIKELY, IMPOSSIBLE.

a) A brontosaurus will walk past a bus stop tomorrow.

b) You will be older tomorrow than today.

c) You will have chips to eat this week.

d) You will learn Chinese at school this year.

e) It will snow in the Sahara desert today.

f) You will have an English lesson tomorrow.

g) An elephant will lay an egg.

h) You will travel in a car this week.

Q2 Karen is playing a wheel of fortune game at a fairground stall. Fill in the missing words, choosing from: CERTAIN, MORE LIKELY, LESS LIKELY, UNLIKELY.

a) She is ..... to win a teddy with her first spin.

b) She is ..... to lose her money than win a prize.

c) She is ..... to win a bar of chocolate than a teddy.

d) She is ..... to win if she has 1 go than if she has 3.

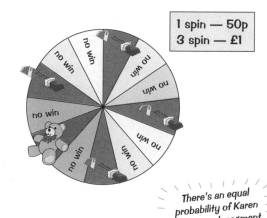

| 1 spin — 50p |
| 3 spin — £1 |

There's an equal probability of Karen getting each segment.

Q3 Think of two events that are:

a) absolutely certain

b) almost certain

c) quite likely

d) have an even chance of happening

e) impossible

Q4 Suzanna has ten cards, numbered 1 to 10. She shuffles them, puts them face down, and then turns them over one at a time.

a) Her first card is a "2". Is the next card likely to be higher or lower? Explain why.

b) The second card she turns over turns out to be a "1". How likely is the next card to be lower? Give reasons for your answer.

Fun in a maths class — it's an impossibility...

Probability can often be about what you think. Like Q1c — you've just got to have a guess at how likely it is you'll eat chips this week. I'm a right unhealthy muck, so for me it's gonna be certain.

Theoretical Probability Problems

Q1 Mark the position of each of these events on this probability scale:

0 _____ 1

a) The probability of the moon exploding tonight.

b) The probability of 1st May being the day after 30th April.

c) The probability of a coin landing on "heads".

d) The probability of getting a five when you roll a six-sided normal die.

e) The probability of getting a heart when you cut a pack of playing cards (without jokers).

f) The probability of a random month NOT beginning with J.

Q2 Brutus is rolling this wacky die.

a) What is the probability that he will roll a prime number?

b) What is the probability that he will roll a multiple of 3?

c) What is the probability that he will roll a factor of 12?

d) What is the probability that he will roll an odd number?

e) What is the probability that he will roll a number greater than 6?

f) What is the probability that he will roll a 1?

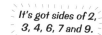

It's got sides of 2, 3, 4, 6, 7 and 9.

Q3 If you have the letters of the word TYRANNOSAURUS, what is the probability of:

a) Choosing a T?

b) Choosing an N?

c) Choosing a P?

d) Choosing a vowel?

Q4 Taissa has 10 cards numbered 1 to 10 face down on the table. She turns one over to see what it is. After she has looked she turns it back and shuffles the cards.

a) What is the probability of getting an even number?

b) What is the probability of getting a 2?

c) What is the probability of getting a 10?

d) What is the probability of getting a multiple of 4?

e) What is the probability of getting a 12?

f) What is the probability of getting a multiple of 3?

Probability Experiments

Q1   Simon and Heather are tossing a coin. They take it in turn to toss 10 times.

a)   Heather gets 7 tails and 3 heads and she says that the coin is biased. Is she right?

b)   Simon throws 10 times and gets 6 tails and 4 heads. Is the coin biased?

c)   They carry on throwing and their results are in the first table. Is the coin really biased? Explain your reasoning.

d)   Savanna and Brian are conducting the same experiment, but with a different coin. Could that coin be biased? Can you be sure?

Simon and Heather	N° of Heads	N° of Tails
after 10 throws	3	7
after 20 throws	7	13
after 50 throws	24	26
after 100 throws	51	49

Savanna and Brian	N° of Heads	N° of Tails
after 10 throws	3	7
after 20 throws	7	13
after 50 throws	16	34
after 100 throws	31	69

Q2   Choose a paragraph from a book or newspaper and count the vowels. Make a table like this:

	a	e	i	o	u
tally					
frequency					

a)   Which is the most common vowel in your sample?

b)   Which is the least frequent?

c)   "e" is the most common vowel in the English language — does your data support this?

d)   If not, what could you do to investigate further?

e)   Find a passage in a foreign language to see which is the most common vowel in that language.

Probability of anyone enjoying homework = 0

Basically the more results you get, the better. Get 2 heads and a tail from 3 tosses and there's not much you can say. But get 200 heads and 100 tails... then you know you've got a dodgy coin.

Experiments v. Theory in Probability

Q1   Fred tosses a fair coin and a fair die.

a)   If he tosses the coin 10 times how many heads should he expect?

b)   If he tosses the coin 100 times how many heads should he expect?

c)   If he tosses the coin 500 times how many heads should he expect?

d)   If he throws the die 6 times how many 3's should he expect?

e)   If he throws the die 60 times how many 3's should he expect?

f)   If he throws the die 300 times how many 3's should he expect?

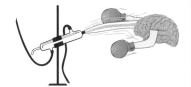

Q2   Eleanor is using this spinner.

a)   What is the probability of it landing on red?

b)   If she spins 10 times how many whites could she expect?

c)   If she spins 100 times how many blues could she expect?

d)   If she spins 500 times how many yellows could she expect?

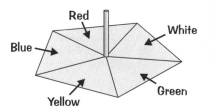

Q3   Georgie has a biased coin. The probability of getting a head is 0.8.

a)   What is the probability of getting a tail?

b)   If she throws the coin 200 times how many heads can she expect?

c)   If she throws the coin 800 times how many tails can she expect?

Q4   Use the random number button on your calculator (ran#) to generate 10 numbers. Each time, note down the second number (the one after the decimal point).

2nd Number	Tally	Frequency
0		
1		
2		
3		
4		
5		
6		
7		
8		
9		

a)   Copy and complete the table on the right.

b)   Describe the frequencies.

Do the same for 20 numbers, and for 50 numbers.

c)   How do the frequencies change (apart from getting bigger)?

In theory, this should probably be quite interesting...

It's the end of the questions. Which means no more work for you... until you get to Year 8.
Imagine how good that'll be — you'll get more work, and the work will be harder. Brilliant.

The Answers

Section One — Numbers and the Number System

Page 1

Q1 a) 9741 (nine thousand seven hundred and forty-one)   1479 (one thousand four hundred and seventy-nine)
    b) 9741. (nine thousand seven hundred and forty-one) .1479 (point one four seven nine)
    c) 9430 (nine thousand four hundred and thirty) 0349 (three hundred and forty-nine)
    d) 9430. (nine thousand four hundred and thirty) .0349 (point nought three four nine)
    e) 87321 (eighty-seven thousand three hundred and twenty-one) 12378 (twelve thousand three hundred and seventy-eight)
    f) 97321 (ninety-seven thousand three hundred and twenty-one) 12379 (twelve thousand three hundred and seventy-nine)

Q2 a) 8 units (8)
    b) 8 tens or eighty (80)
    c) 8 tenths (0.8)
    d) 8 hundredths (0.08)
    e) 80 thousands or 8 ten-thousands (80 000)
    f) 8 thousandths (0.008)
    g) 8 hundreds (800)
    h) 8 hundred thousands (800 000)
    i) 8 thousands (8 000)

Q3 a) £6.90
    b) £2.02
    c) £1.54
    d) £2.37

Q4 a) 1.6, 1.7, 1.8, 1.9
    b) 6.18, 6.19, 6.20, 6.21
    c) 9.0, 8.9, 8.8, 8.7
    d) 0.52, 0.51, 0.50, 0.49

Q5 a) 340
    b) 3.4
    c) 0.27
    d) 3.4
    e) 27
    f) 340
    parts a) and f), and b) and d) have the same answer.

Q6 a) 0.01
    b) 0.01
    c) 0.01
    d) 100

Page 2

Q1 a) 1.3, 1.5, 1.54, 1.62, 1.71, 1.89, 1.98
    b) 100.3, 100.4, 100.43, 101.2, 101.6, 102.8, 102.89
    c) -10, -3, -1, 0, 2, 4, 5
    d) 7.09, 7.13, 7.18, 7.21, 7.36, 7.40, 7.41

Q2 a) 4.1 cm, 4.0 cm, 3.9 cm, 3.1 cm, 2.3 cm, 2 cm, 0.9 cm
    b) 79.1 km, 78.7 km, 76.1 km, 75.2 km, 74.9 km, 74.3 km, 74.1 km
    c) 0.220 m, 0.219 m, 0.102 m, 0.021 m, 0.02 m, 0.012 m, 0.009 m
    d) 41.1 g, 41.06 g, 40.93 g, 40.81 g, 40.73 g, 40.7 g, 40.07 g

Q3 a) >
    b) <
    c) <
    d) =
    e) >
    f) >

Q4 Many possible answers

Q5 a) 0.015
    b) 4.35
    c) 101.75
    d) 0.05
    e) 3.25
    f) -3.15

Q6 a) 8, 9, 10, 11
    b) 103, 104, 105, 106, 107
    c) 224, 225, 226, 227, 228
    d) 24, 25, 26, 27, 28

Page 3

Q1 a) 10 °C
    b) 14 °C
    c) 31 °C
    d) 8 °C
    e) 6 °C

Q2 a) floor 4
    b) floor 6
    c) floor 0 (ground)
    d) floor -1 (basement)

Q3 a) owes 50p
    b) owes £4.75
    c) has £1.50

Q4 4210m

Q5 Shane 7 years, Henry 4 years. Or Shane 12 years, Henry 9 years. Or any other answer, where Shane's age is 3 years greater than Henry's.

Q6

-5	2	-6
-4	-3	-2
0	-8	-1

-5	3	-4
-1	-2	-3
0	-7	1

-7	4	0
6	-1	-8
-2	-6	5

Page 4

Q1 a) (i) 6.13   (ii) 6.1   (iii) 6
    b) (i) 5.91   (ii) 5.9   (iii) 6
    c) (i) 0.06   (ii) 0.1   (iii) 0
    d) (i) 11.96   (ii) 12.0   (iii) 12
    e) (i) 0.98   (ii) 1.0   (iii) 1
    f) (i) 1.20   (ii) 1.2   (iii) 1

Q2 a) 30.07
    b) 3816
    c) 83.5
    d) 39.78
    e) 6.4
    f) 0.054

Q3 60 × 3 = 180 kg.

Q4 a) 2 packs
    b) 8 bottles
    c) 7 packs
    d) 3 packs
    e) 5 bags of crisps, 5 glasses of cola, 3 sausage rolls, 2 chocolate bars

Q5 64 tiles (you don't want gaps in the carpet)

Page 5

Q1 $3^2 = 9$, $1^3 = 1$, $64 = 4^3$, $0 = 0^3$, $\sqrt{100} = 10$, $8 = 2^3$, $7 = \sqrt{49}$, $36 = 6^2$

Q2 b) 3 and 4
    c) 2 and 3

Q3 a) 169
    b) 17
    c) 0.008
    d) 6.859
    e) 1.69
    f) 3.2
    g) 39601
    h) 7.7

Q4 1, 4, 9, 16, 25, 36, 49, 64, 81, 100, 121, 144, 169
    9 + 16 = 25   36 + 64 = 100
    25 + 144 = 169

Q5 a)
    b) 3   5   25
    c) always add up to a square number

The Answers

Page 6

Q1   2, 3, 5, 7, 11, 13, 17, 19, 23, 29

Q2   a)   1, 2, 5, 10
      b)   1, 2, 4, 7, 14, 28
      c)   1, 7
      d)   1, 2, 3, 4, 6, 8, 12, 16, 24, 48
      e)   1, 2, 3, 4, 6, 8, 9, 12, 18, 24,
            36, 72
      f)   1, 5, 25
      g)   1, 2, 5, 7, 10, 14, 35, 70
      h)   1, 2, 3, 6, 7, 14, 21, 42
      i)   1, 2, 3, 4, 5, 6, 9, 10, 12, 15,
            18, 20, 30, 36, 45, 60, 90, 180

Q3   a)   5
      b)   14
      c)   4
      d)   36

Q4   a)   24
      b)   24
      c)   18
      d)   72

Q5

1	2	3	4	5	6	7	8	9	10
11	12	13	14	15	16	17	18	19	20
21	22	23	24	25	26	27	28	29	30
31	32	33	34	35	36	37	38	39	40
41	42	43	44	45	46	47	48	49	50
51	52	53	54	55	56	57	58	59	60
61	62	63	64	65	66	67	68	69	70
71	72	73	74	75	76	77	78	79	80
81	82	83	84	85	86	87	88	89	90
91	92	93	94	95	96	97	98	99	100

Q6   a)   7
      b)   12
      c)   80
      d)   9
      e)   2
      f)   4

Q7

×	6	3
2	12	6
11	66	33

×	8	36
3	24	108
4	32	144

or

×	4	18
6	24	108
8	32	144

or

×	2	9
12	24	108
16	32	144

Page 7

Q1   a) 3^4
      b) 4^5
      c) 10^7
      d) 25^2

Q2   a) 2^3
      b) 3^3
      c) 4^2
      d) 2^4
      e) 10^3
      f) 5^3

Q3   a) $2 \times 2 \times 3$
      b) $2 \times 2 \times 3 \times 3$
      c) $2 \times 3 \times 7$
      d) $3 \times 5 \times 5$
      e) $2 \times 3 \times 3 \times 7$
      f) $2 \times 2 \times 11$
      g) $2 \times 3 \times 3 \times 3$
      h) $2 \times 2 \times 5 \times 5$

Q4   a) $2^2 \times 3$
      b) $2^2 \times 3^2$
      c) $2 \times 3 \times 7$
      d) 3×5^2
      e) $2 \times 3^2 \times 7$
      f) $2^2 \times 11$
      g) 2×3^3
      h) $2^2 \times 5^2$

Q5 $10^2 = 100$ $10^3 = 1000$
      $1000000 = 10^6$ $10^1 = 10$
      $100000 = 10^5$

Q6 10^3

Q7 10^5

Page 8

Q1   a)   1/2 = 3/6 = 6/12 = 2/4 = 20/40
            = 50/100 = 250/500
      b)   1/3 = 4/12 = 3/9 = 30/90 = 7/21
            = 10/30 = 300/900
      c)   1/5 = 2/10 = 20/100 = 4/20
            = 7/35 = 40/200 = 100/500
      d)   3/7 = 6/14 = 9/21 = 21/49
            = 12/28 = 60/140 = 150/350

Q2   a)   1/3
      b)   1/4
      c)   4/5
      d)   4/9
      e)   3/7
      f)   1/10

Q3   a)   2½
      b)   3½
      c)   2 1/7
      d)   2½
      e)   2¼
      f)   3 3/5

Q4   a)   5/2
      b)   5/4
      c)   16/5
      d)   16/7
      e)   53/10
      f)   35/8

Q5

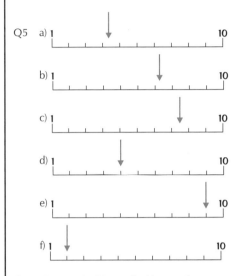

Q6   Noreen 12, Norma 5, Norman 3

Q7   3/4, since 3/4 = 6/8 which is more than
      5/8

Page 9

Q1   a)   0.5
      b)   0.25
      c)   0.125
      d)   0.0625
      e)   0.75
      f)   0.375
      g)   0.1
      h)   0.3
      i)   0.15

Q2   a)   0.5
      b)   0.25
      c)   0.2
      d)   0.4
      e)   0.15
      f)   0.12
      g)   0.14
      h)   0.78
      i)   0.52

Q3   a)   50%
      b)   25%
      c)   75%
      d)   30%
      e)   15%
      f)   80%
      g)   12%
      h)   28%

Q4   a)   0.1 = 1/10
      b)   0.2 = 1/5
      c)   0.25 = 1/4
      d)   0.3 = 3/10
      e)   0.7 = 7/10
      f)   0.8 = 4/5
      g)   1.5 = 3/2
      h)   2.25 = 9/4

The Answers

Q5 a) 0.125
b) 0.188 (3 d.p.)
c) 0.143 (3 d.p.)
d) 0.273 (3 d.p.)
e) 0.145
f) 0.115
g) 0.333 (3 d.p.)
h) 0.667 (3 d.p.)

Q6 1/9 = 0.1111111, 2/9 = 0.22222222
etc.
So they're all the number recurring e.g.
5/9 would be 0.55555555

Page 10

Q1 a) 1/4, 3/8, 1/2, 5/8, 3/4
b) 1/16, 3/16, 3/8, 5/8, 3/4, 15/16
c) 1/6, 1/3, 1/2, 2/3, 5/6, 1
d) 1/2, 2/3, 3/4, 4/5, 5/6
e) 1/100, 1/50, 7/100, 3/25, 3/10
f) 19/25, 77/100, 39/50, 23/25

Q2 a) e.g. 3/8
b) e.g. 1/6
c) e.g. 9/10
d) e.g. 1/2
e) e.g. 11/16
f) e.g. 9/20
g) e.g. 9/100
h) e.g. 3/4

Q3 a) 7/10, 50%, 0.4
b) 80%, 0.7, 3/5
c) 9/20, 35%, 0.33
d) 99%, 0.91, 9/10
e) 0.11, 10%, 1/11
f) 1/3, 33%, 0.04
g) 4/10, 0.39, 4%
h) 53.5% , 0.531, 13/25

Q4 1/4 = 4/16 = 25%
22/40 = 11/20 = 55%
1/5 of 200 = 160/4 = 40
1/16 × 8 = 50% = 8 ÷ 16

Q5 a) £2250
b) £2250

Q6 3/16

Page 11

Q1 a) 1/4
b) 1/8
c) 1/4
d) 1/4
e) 1/2
f) 1/4

Q2 a) 1/3
b) 1/6
c) 1/8
d) 1/8
e) 1/5

Q3 Pupil's own answers

Q4 a) 2m
b) 34 kg
c) £4
d) 1/2
e) 3.2
f) £3

Page 12

Q1 10% of 50, 1/5 of 25
50% of 8, 32 ÷8
40% of 200, 0.2 × 400
810 ÷9, 450 × 1/5
1/3 of 57, 0.25 ×76
16 × 1/8, 1% of 200
72 × 1/6, 10% of 120

Q2 a) 200
b) 50
c) 25
d) 6
e) 5
f) 9
g) 8
h) 36

Q3 a) £3.40
b) 50p
c) 5p
d) 75p
e) 60 cm
f) 6 mm
g) 500 m
h) 50 m

Q4 a) £6.50
b) 9.03 m
c) £44.44
d) 20.25 kg
e) £28.22
f) 620 g
g) £42.94
h) 491.4 g

Q5 25% of his house number (28) is 7. 3
times the number of vehicles (3) is 9
She should choose three times the
number of vehicles.

Page 13

Q1 1 1/4, 3/4, 0.25, 0.75, 25%,
       75%, 3:1
    2 1/3, 2/3, 0.333, 0.667, 33.3%,
       66.6%, 2:1
    3 1/2, 1/2, 0.5, 0.5, 50%, 50%, 1:1
    4 1/4, 3/4, 0.25, 0.75, 25%,
       75%, 3:1
    5 3/10, 7/10, 0.3, 0.7, 30%,
       70%, 7:3
    6 3/5, 2/5, 0.6, 0.4, 3:2
    7 1/5, 4/5, 0.2, 0.8, 20%,
       80%, 4:1

Q2 18

Q3 2

Q4 15

Q5 60 oranges, 20 mangoes, 40 peaches

Q6 a) 12
b) 6
c) 24 sandwiches. 1 egg will be left
over.

Page 14

Q1 a) 1:2
b) 1:3
c) 2:3
d) 1:2
e) 1:4
f) 8:1
g) 3:1
h) 1:5

Q2 a) £4, £4
b) £2, £4
c) £3, £9
d) £20, £4
e) £80, £20
f) £25, £75
g) £1, 50p
h) £3, £21

Q3 a) 400
b) 500
c) 40

Q4 a) 7:6
b) 27
c) 3:4
d) 1:1
e) boys:girls = 11:5, girls:boys = 5:11

Q5 a) 1:1
b) 1:2
c) 1:4

Section Two — Calculations

Page 15

Q1 a) 144
b) 270
c) 817
d) 2277
e) 3567
f) 356.7

Q2 a = d
b = f
c = e

Q3 a) 220
b) 98
c) 350
d) 320
e) 5
f) 30

Q4 a) 14 (e.g. 14 × 8 = 112)
b) 15 (e.g. 14 × 15 = 210)
c) 18 (e.g. 18 × 21 = 378)
d) 51 (e.g. 51 × 21 = 1071)
e) 12 (e.g. 12 × 17 = 204)
f) 160 (e.g. 160 × 15 = 2400

The Answers

Q5 a) i) 6 r 1   ii) 6 1/4   iii) 6.25
    b) i) 5 r 3   ii) 5 1/4   iii) 5.25
    c) i) 11 r 3, ii) 11 3/8, iii) 11.375
    d) i) 10 r 4, ii) 10 1/10,iii) 10.1
    e) i) 15 r 1, ii) 15 1/6, iii) 15.17
    f) i) 22 r 1, ii) 22 1/3, iii) 22.33

Q6 1/4 of 12.8= 25.6 × 1/8 = 19.2/6 = 3.2
    1, 3, and 4 have the same value.

Q7 626 ÷ 6 = 104 remainder 2

Page 16

Q1 a) 22
    b) 42
    c) 10
    d) 35
    e) 30
    f) 36
    g) 21
    h) 23.25
    i) 0.75

Q2 a) 5 (3 left)
    b) 4 (1 left)
    c) 3 (3 left)
    d) 3 (6 left)

Q3 a) 12 (4 left)
    b) 18 (4 left)
    c) 14 (8 left)
    d) 7 (8 left)

Q4 a) 15
    b) 9
    c) 6
    d) 6

Q5 a) 13
    b) 9
    c) 10
    d) 10
    e) 11. 60 − 2 = 58. 632 ÷ 58 = 10.9.

Q6 a) £14396.33
    b) 220.9 kg (or 221 kg)
    c) 0.01 m or 1 cm
    d) 0.625
    e) 10 (38 sweets left)
    f) 20 minutes or 0.33 hours (2 d.p.)

Page 17

Q1 a) 54
    b) 29
    c) 33
    d) 0.3
    e) 0.6
    f) 0.18
    g) 8.7
    h) 2.3
    i) 5.5

Q2 a) 1280
    b) 87.2
    c) 620
    d) 167.3
    e) 4700
    f) 1160
    g) 24445
    h) 1180
    i) 1972

Q3 a) 9
    b) 6
    c) 10
    d) 25
    e) 8
    f) 4
    g) 20
    h) 21

Q4 a) 100, 1, 0.01
    b) 9, 900, 0.09
    c) 81, 0.81, 8100
    d) 6, 0.6, 60
    e) 0.4
    f) 0.8
    g) 27
    h) 125
    i) 2

Q5

Fraction	1/2	1/4	1/5	1/10	3/20	1 1/4	1 ¾	1/8	$\frac{1}{100}$	$2\frac{1}{10}$
Decimal	0.5	0.25	0.2	0.1	0.15	1.25	1.75	0.125	0.01	2.1
Percentage	50%	25%	20%	10%	15%	125%	175%	12.5%	1%	210%

Q6 a) 2 hr = 120 min = 7200 sec
    b) 1 wk = 7 days = 168 hr
    c) 3 km = 3000 m = 300 000cm
    d) 5.5 m = 550 cm = 5500 mm
    e) 5 miles is approx 8 km
    f) 2.5 kg = 2500 g
    g) 1 kg is approx 2.2 lb
    h) 1 gallon is approx 4½ litres

Page 18

Q1 a) 31
    b) 61
    c) 83
    d) 102
    e) 93
    f) 72
    g) 152
    h) 38
    i) 35

Q2 a) 11.9
    b) 10.4
    c) 3.9
    d) 7.1
    e) 13.6
    f) 9.38
    g) 0.44
    h) 1.98
    i) 0.04

Q3 a) 6
    b) -9
    c) 10
    d) 5
    e) 0
    f) 0
    g) -300
    h) -1000

Q4 a) 3
    b) 2
    c) 0.2
    d) 0.02
    e) 0.03
    f) 0.02

Q5 10

Q6 74

Q7 26.5 m

Page 19

Q1 a) 11
    b) 11
    c) 235
    d) 1482
    e) 50
    f) 3650
    g) 1.16
    h) 0.166

Q2 a) 97
    b) 7.4
    c) 6.3
    d) 525
    e) 754
    f) 1.54
    g) 3488
    h) 0.2134

Q3 a) 18.3
    b) 149
    c) 0.35
    d) 1871
    e) 8645
    f) 0.073
    g) 0.36
    h) 9.9

Q4 a) 58
    b) 19.8
    c) 0.083
    d) 6.43
    e) 11.87
    f) 0.0141
    g) 84.1
    h) 8.3

Q5 Burgers and two of chips, chocolate cake and orange. OR chips, chocolate cake, and orange squash.

Q6 Bag of toffees and 2 chocolate bars (giving 42 pence change), OR chocolate bar, bottle of cola and ice cream (giving 54 pence change) OR toffees and ice cream (giving 42 pence change) OR toffees and cola (giving 41 pence change).

The Answers

Page 20

Q1 a) 28 000
b) 2350
c) 310 000
d) 23.5
e) 68
f) 0.11
g) 1.72
h) 0.144

Q2 a) 27.6
b) 137.6
c) 717.1
d) 183.6
e) 1560
f) 82 410
g) 2277
h) 7920

Q3 a) 270
b) 700
c) 3200
d) 700
e) 47 000
f) 72 000
g) 76
h) 3.2

Q4 a) 938.6
b) 0.17
c) 64.6
d) 1626.9
e) 3.8
f) 6.12
g) 29
h) 3.4

Q5 0.3125 m = 31.25 cm = 312.5 mm

Page 21

Q1 a) 0.8
b) 0.7
c) 1.25
d) 0.375
e) 0.56
f) 3/25
g) 0.48
h) 0.17

Q2 a) 0.27
b) 15/100 = 3/20, 15%
c) 0.45, 45/100 = 9/20
d) 0.73, 73%
e) 1.2, 120/100 = $1\frac{1}{5}$
f) 0.05, 5%
g) 4/5, 80%
h) 1.7, 170%

Q3 a) 21
b) 62
c) 4
d) 33
e) 12
f) 25
g) 32
h) 150

Q4 Farzana £1.80, Ahmed £2.40,
Tariq 72p, Dad £2.28

Q5 2 1/5 = 22/10 = 2 2/10
4/7 = 8/14 = 20/35
4/100 = 2/50 = 1/25
34/10 = 17/5 = 3 2/5
3/5 = 60/100 = 24/40
5 1/5 = 26/5 = 52/10
3/20 = 9/60 = 27/180
2/3 = 40/60 = 30/45

Page 22

Q1 a) £10.40
b) £9.80
c) £18.20
d) £18.75
e) £13.50
f) £21.20

Q2 a) £6.30
b) £5.60
c) £16.00
d) £5.46
e) £1.47
f) £8.97

Q3 a) (7 + 6) − 4 = 9
b) 7 × 6 + 4 = 46
c) 7 × (6 + 4) = 70
d) (7 + 6) × 4 = 52
e) (7 − 4) × 6 = 18
f) 7 × 6 × 4 = 168
g) 7 − 6 − 4 = -3
h) 7 × 6 ÷ 4 = 10.5

Q4 variations of:

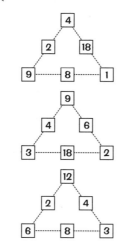

Page 23

Q1 a) 1613
b) 5005
c) 78
d) 1038
e) 7271
f) 7279
g) 1890
h) 10 440

Q2 a) 14 742
b) 4572
c) 7856
d) 7614
e) 13 373
f) 30 492
g) 47 268
h) 10 989

Q3 a) 41.82
b) 241.06
c) 9.912
d) 10.802
e) 1.4212
f) 77.38
g) 71.427
h) 62.46

Q4 a) £33.72
b) £29.21
c) £42.51
d) £238.70
e) £78.40
f) £30.87
g) £31.96
h) £485.37

Page 24

Q1 a) £5.65
b) £25.40
c) £31.58
d) £19.25
e) £56.40
f) £34.60
g) £83.50
h) £41.25

Q2 a) 23
b) 17
c) 21
d) 49
e) 33
f) 51
g) 29
h) 42

Q3 a) 56 r 1
b) 23 r 3
c) 31 r 11
d) 19 r 6
e) 11 r 20
f) 3 r 12
g) 13 r 2
h) 12 r 6

Q4 a) 20.7
b) 22.9
c) 24.7
d) 31.3
e) 37.8
f) 9.1
g) 5.9
h) 27.8

Q5 a) 7 buses
b) 9 minibuses
c) 13 planes

The Answers

Page 25

Q1 a) £42.38
   b) £237.15
   c) £4.05
   d) £61.08
   e) £66.67
   f) 90p
   g) 53p
   h) £333.33

Q2 a) 34.5 hr = 34 hr 30 min
   b) 23.5 hr = 23 hr 30 min
   c) 12.5 hr = 12 hr 30 min
   d) 6.25 hr = 6 hr 15 min
   e) 7.25 hr = 7 hr 15 min
   f) 8.4 hr = 8 hr 24 min
   g) 1 1/3 hr = 1 hr 20 min
   h) 1.5 hr = 1hr 30 min

Q3 a) 6/7
   b) 2/3
   c) 1/5
   d) 3/5
   e) 1 1/4
   f) 1 1/2
   g) 2 1/4
   h) 1 2/9

Q4 a) 1 3/14
   b) 7/55
   c) 2/7
   d) 2 4/7
   e) 2 1/6
   f) 2 27/32
   g) 25 1/5
   h) 8 1/24

Q5 a) £25.33
   b) £9.50
   c) £12.67

Page 26

Q1 a) 441
   b) 1806.25
   c) 0.1681
   d) 16
   e) 27
   f) 0.01
   g) 25
   h) 85

Q2 a) -37.5
   b) -191.7
   c) -12
   d) -10.4
   e) 11.48
   f) 4.3

Q3 a) 23
   b) 17
   c) 6
   d) 4
   e) 2.5
   f) 2

Q4 a) 89.6
   b) 75.6
   c) 15.5
   d) 53.94
   e) 20
   f) 108.92
   g) 16.25
   h) 58.656

Q5 a) $0.\dot{1}$
   b) $0.\dot{2}$
   c) $0.\dot{3}$
   d) $0.\dot{4}$

It's just $0.\dot{n}$, where n is the number at the top of the fractions (numerator).

Page 27

Q1 a) correct
   b) wrong 35.7
   c) wrong -20.61
   d) correct
   e) wrong 145
   f) correct
   g) wrong 1.5
   h) correct

Q2 a) correct
   b) wrong £2.06
   c) wrong £12.68
   d) wrong £109.01
   e) wrong 1.5 hr = 1 hr 30 min
   f) correct
   g) wrong 1.38 km
   h) wrong 5220 g

Q3 a) 16
   b) 69
   c) 3.1
   d) 666
   e) 622
   f) 2.5
   g) 81
   h) 3

Q4 a) correct
   b) correct
   c) wrong 3721
   d) correct
   e) wrong 0.0125
   f) wrong 1 17/24
   g) correct
   h) wrong 26.42

Section Three — Solving Problems

Page 28

Q1 a) £61.20
   b) £47.10
   c) £182.00

Q2 a) 4 × £12.99 = £51.96
   b) 40 for £9 (22 1/2p each)
   c) 5 for £8.50 (£1.70 each)
   d) 10 for £3.99 (39.9p each)
   e) 3 for £3.99 (£1.33 each)

Q3 a) £1500
   b) 10%
   c) 83 1/3 % or 83.3% to 1 d.p.
   d) 5% off bill - saves £75

Q4 a) 20 cm × 32 cm
   b) 10 cm × 16 cm
   c) 160 cm^2

Q5 115 cm = 1.15 m

Page 29

Q1 a) sweets £6, going out £6, saving £3
   b) £4
   c) 8 weeks (£32)

Q2 900 FF
   £10.40

Q3 290 000 lire

Q4 a) butter 300 g, flour 450 g, cocoa 240 g, eggs 12, walnuts 300 g, sugar 1350 g.
   b) 100 brownies

Q5 a) 5:4
   b) 432
   c) 240 blue, 192 white

Page 30

Q1 a) (i) 9876 – 01 = 9875
      (ii) 0123 – 98 = 25
   b) (i) 9875 + 64 or 9874 + 65 or 9864 + 75 etc. = 9939
      (ii) 0124 + 35 or 0125 + 34 = 159
   c) (i) 876 × 9 = 7884
      (ii) 013 × 2 = 26
   d) (i) 87654 × 9 = 788 886
      (ii) 02345 × 1 = 02345
   e) (i) 96 × 87 = 8352
      (ii) 01 × 23 = 23
   f) (i) 987 ÷ 1 = 987
      (ii) 012 ÷ 9 = 1.333 3 d.p.
   g) (i) 98 ÷ 01 = 98
      (ii) 01 ÷ 98 = 0.010 3 d.p.
   h) (i) 97531 + 86420 = 183 951 (or equiv)
      (ii) 13579 + 02468 = 16 047 (or equiv)

Q2 a) + ÷
   b) – ÷
   c) × –
   d) × –
   e) + ×
   f) – ×
   g) – –
   h) – +

Q3 a) 0
   b) 1
   c) 2
   d) 50

The Answers

e)   9
f)   19
g)   29
h)   99

Q4   a)   54
     b)   63
     c)   72
     d)   81
     e)   90
     f)   99

Q5   a)   n x 2
     b)   n - 3

Page 31

Q1   a)   16 cm
     b)   26 m
     c)   20 cm
     d)   12.8 cm or 128 mm
     e)   7 m or 700 cm
          P = 2a + 2b or P = 2(a + b)

Q2   a)   5 and 6
     b)   10 and 11
     c)   15 and 16
     d)   20 and 21
     e)   31 and 32
     f)   72 and 73
     g)   1004 and 1005
     No, because one number must be odd.

Q3   a)   9 and 11
     b)   49 and 51
     c)   249 and 251
     d)   499 and 501
     e)   2749 and 2751
     f)   -1 and -3
          Yes

Q4   a)   £51.80
     b)   C equals 2 lots of £14.50 and 3
          lots of £7.60 (or equivalent)
     c)   C = 14.50 x + 7.60 y

Q5   a)   19, 31
     b)   18, 30
     c)   18, 60

Page 32

Q1
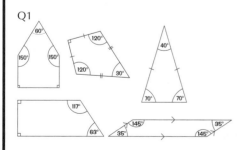

Q2   a)   28
     b)   20
     c)   112

Q3   a)   No. Isosceles triangles have to have
          2 equal angle, and angles of a
          triangle add up to 180°

Q4   a)   1
     b)   5
     c)   14

Q5   a)   680 m²
     b)   52 m²
     c)   46 m
     d)   104 m

Page 33

Q1   b)

     c)

     d)

Q2
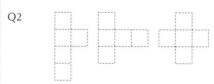

     Other sensible answers accepted.

Q3   81 m²

Q4   36 cm

Q5   a)   4.5 cm²
     b)   20 cm²

Q6   a)   1/3, 2/3
     b)   1/8, 7/8

Page 34

Q1   a)   1/6
     b)   0
     c)   1
     d)   26/52 = 1/2
     e)   4/52 = 1/13
     f)   3/6 = 1/2
     g)   11/20
     h)   19/100

Q2   a)   20/100 = 1/5
     b)   2/100 = 1/50
     c)   54/100 = 27/50
     d)   (i) 1 (ii) 2   (iii) 20
     e)   (£5 × 100) – (£200 × 2) = £100

Q3   a)   Correct 1/5 = 0.2
     b)   Incorrect 4/5 = 0.8

Page 35

Q1   a)   (i)   12 × 1 perimeter 104 cm
          (ii)   4 × 3 perimeter 56 cm

Q2   a)   12.9 cm² or 1290 mm²
     b)   2.601 m² or 26010 cm²
     c)   0.11 m² or 1100 cm²

Q3   a)   12 years
     b)   Brian 16, Clara 14, Delores 8
     c)   5 times
     d)   Brian 12, Delores 4
     e)   3 times

Q4   a)   5
     b)   5
     c)   20
     d)   20

Q5   Pupil's methods will vary
     a)   22.65
     b)   £21.00
     c)   160.7
     d)   £1.47
     e)   £15.92

Page 36

Q1   a)   6
     b)   24

Q2   3 cm × 10 = 30 cm

Q3   All amounts possible from 1p to £3.88
     EXCEPT the following:
     14p, 19p, 24p, 29p, 34p, 39p-49p incl,
     54p, 59p, 64p, 69p, 74p, 79p, 84p, 89p-
     99p incl plus all these with £1, £2, £3

Q4   a)   2   5   14   41   122
     b)   1   2   5   14   41
     c)   0   -1   -4   -13   -40
     d)   -2   -7   -22   -67   -202

Q5   a)   2   4   16   256   65536
     b)   1   1   1   1   1
     c)   -2   4   16   256   65536
     d)   0.5   0.25   0.0625   0.00391
     e)   0.1   0.01   0.0001   0.000 000 01

Page 37

Q1   a)   difference between products
          always 10
     b)   difference between products
          always 40
     c)   difference between products
          always 20 (2 rows, 3 columns)

Q2   The difference between the products is
     the square number × 10, e.g. :-
     2 × 10 → 10
     3 × 10 → 40
     4 × 10 → 90
     (n – 1)² × 10 → product

The Answers

Q3 missing numbers (top row first)
- a) 90, 32
- b) 35, 20, 9, 6
- c) 44.1, 20.2, 6.4, 10.1
- d) 72, 48, 4
- e) 2160000, 4800, 30, 16
- f) 2, 1, 1

Page 38

Q1 1
1,2
1,3
1,2,4
1,5
1,2,3,6
1,7
1,2,4,8
1,3,9
1,2,5,10
1,11
1,2,3,4,6,12
1,13
1,2,7,14
1,3,5,15
1,2,4,8,16
1,17
1,2,3,6,9,18
1,19
1,2,4,5,10,20
- a) 1,2,3,5,7,11,13,17,19 prime (except 1)
- b) 1,4,9,16 square
- c) all square numbers have an odd number of factors

Q2
- a) 31
- b) 151
- c) 3 × number of pens +1

Q3
- a) 52
- b) 252
- c) (5 × number of pairs of pens)+2

Q4
- a) 64 pens, 125 hurdles
- b) 74 pens, 145 hurdles

Section Four — Algebra

Page 39

Q1
- a) a = 4
- b) b = 4
- c) c = 5
- d) d = 5
- e) e = 6
- f) f = 26
- g) g = 14
- h) h = 2

Q2
- a) 3j
- b) 5k
- c) 3m + n + p
- d) 5q
- e) 6r
- f) 3s
- g) 2(t + u)
- h) 7w + 3v

Q3
- a) true
- b) false
- c) false
- d) false
- e) false
- f) true

Q4
- a) 3x = 24, x = 8
- b) w/7 = 3, w = 21
- c) 5z + 7 = 52, z = 9
- d) x^2 = 36, x = 6 (or -6)
- e) 4(n + 3) = 28, n = 4
- f) 3(n/3 + 3) = 15, n = 6
- g) p – s = t, where p = pocket money, s = spent money, t = saved money
- h) s – b = p, where s = selling price, b = buying price, p = profit

Page 40

Q1
- a) 1
- b) 2.5
- c) 13.75
- d) 0.35
- e) -3
- f) -5
- g) 4
- h) 6

Q2
- a) 3
- b) 0.5
- c) 5
- d) 11
- e) 15
- f) -6
- g) 10
- h) -4

Q3 12 × (3 + 4) = (12 × 3) + (12 × 4)
12 – (3 + 4) = 12 – 3 – 4
12 – (3 – 4) = 12 – 3 + 4
a(b – c) = ab – ac
ab + c = c + ba
a – (b + c) = a – b – c
a – (b – c) = a – b + c

Q4
- a) m = 9
- b) n = 12
- c) r = 0
- d) s = 2

Page 41

Q1
- a) 4a
- b) 3b + 2c
- c) 4d + e + 3f
- d) 2 + 2g
- e) 1
- f) $5j^2 + 3j$
- g) -2n
- h) 16p – 13q – 4r

Q2
- a) 3z – 12
- b) 7y +5
- c) 8w – 45
- d) 14v +10u
- e) 3t – 26 s
- f) 3r + 6s – 9t
- g) 10q + 6n
- h) 8m – 10k + 8

Q3
- a) 6g +14
- b) 6b
- c) 4h + 12
- d) 4d + 14
- e) 5e – 2
- f) 2a + 6
- g) 12f

Q4
- a) 6 m × 6 m
- b) 4 m × 8 m
- c) 5 m × 7 m
- d) 1 m × 11 m
- e) 3 m × 9 m
- f) 2 m × 10 m

Page 42

Q1
- a) $j = 5$
- b) $k = 5$
- c) $m = 11$
- d) $n = 5$
- e) $p = 5$
- f) $q = 18$
- g) $r = 4$
- h) $s = 1.4$

Q2
- a) $x = 2$
- b) $x = 4$
- c) $x = 2$
- d) $x = 6$
- e) $x = 0.5$
- f) $x = 4$
- g) $x = 12$
- h) $x = 3$

Q3 7a + 23 = 44
→ 7a = 21
→ a = 3

Q4
- a) c = 300 x 16 + 200
  c = 5000 ml = 5 litres
- b) 12 cups
- c) 200 ml

Q5
- a) 17x = 102cm x = 6 cm
- b) (6 × 5) + (4 × 4) + 3 = 49
- c) 45+6x = 63, x =3

Page 43

Q1
- a) 2, 3, 4, 5, 6 whole numbers (starting at 2)
- b) 2, 4, 6, 8, 10 2 times table (even numbers)
- c) 3, 5, 7, 9, 11 odd numbers
- d) 3, 6, 9, 12, 15 3 times table
- e) 1.5, 2, 2.5, 3, 3.5 up in halves
- f) 0, 3, 6, 9, 12 3 times table
- g) 5, 10, 15, 20, 25 5 times table
- h) 9, 8, 7, 6, 5 down by 1

Q2
- a) 10 cm^2
- b) 30 cm^2
- c) 3 m
- d) 8 km

Q3
- a) £15 = 1500 p
- b) £b = (8n + 1500)/100
- c) £16.60
- d) £24.60
- e) £19.80

The Answers

Q4 a) £x = (50d + 25e)/100, where *d* =
            number daytime calls, and
            e = number of evening calls
    b) £12.50
    c) £27.50
    d) 92
    e) 8

Page 44

Q1 a) add 2 (odd numbers); 9,11
    b) add 2; 303, 305
    c) subtract 3; 11, 8
    d) add 4; 20, 24
    e) add 7; 40, 47
    f) subtract 2; 0, -2
    g) × by 2; 96, 192
    h) divide by 2; 16, 8

Q2 a) 19, 28
    b) 38, 54
    c) 4, 32
    d) 4, 1/2
    e) 0, -10
    f) 21, 54
    g) 54, 27, 9, 0
    h) 9, 81

Q3 a) 3, 5, 7, 9, 11
    b) 1, 4, 7, 10, 13
    c) 2, 7, 12. 17, 22
    d) 12, 13, 14, 15, 16
    e) 3, 13, 23, 33, 43
    f) 2, 1, 0, -1, -2
    g) ½, 1, 1½, 2, 2½
    h) 3½, 4, 4½, 5, 5½

Q4 a) 21, 34
    b) 29, 47
    c) 45, 73

Page 45

Q1 a) 2, 5, 8, 11, 14, 17
    b) 7, 6, 5, 4, 3, 2
    c) 4, 11, 18, 25, 32, 39
    d) 100, 85, 70, 55, 40, 25
    e) 4, 12, 36, 108, 324, 972
    f) 800, 400, 200, 100, 50, 25
    g) 3, 30, 300, 3000, 30 000, 300 000
    h) 6, 3, 0, -3, -6, -9

Q2 a) 2, 4, 6, 8, 10, 12
    b) 5, 7, 9, 11, 13, 15
    c) 6, 8, 10, 12, 14, 16
    d) 1, 3, 5, 7, 9, 11
    e) 3, 6, 9, 12, 15, 18
    f) 6, 9, 12, 15, 18, 21
    g) 7, 10, 13, 16, 19, 22
    h) 2, 5, 8, 11, 14, 17

Q3 a) 3, 7, 12, 52
    b) 3, 15, 30, 150
    c) 3, 11, 21, 101
    d) -1, 3, 8, 48
    e) 10, 50, 100, 500
    f) 1, 17, 37, 197
    g) 99, 95, 90, 50
    h) 98, 90, 80, 0

Q4 a) 4, 8, 12, 16, 20
    b) 2, 5, 8, 11, 14
    c) 10, 8, 6, 4, 2
    d) 20, 22, 24, 26, 28
    e) 10, 8, 6, 4, 2
    f) 20, 22, 24, 26, 28
    g) 4, 8, 12, 16, 20
    h) 2, 5, 8, 11, 14
    a) = g)
    b) = h)
    c) = e)
    d) = f)

Page 46

Q1

4	5	6
⬚⬚⬚	⬚⬚⬚⬚	⬚⬚⬚⬚⬚

    b) 31
    c) 301
    d) multiply n by 3 and add 1
    e) 3n + 1

Q2

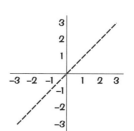

    b) 30
    c) 300
    d) multiply n by 3
    e) 3n

Q3

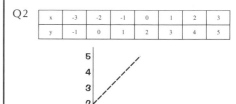

    b) 30
    c) 300
    d) multiply n by 3
    e) 3n

Q4

    b) 100
    c) 10 000
    d) square n (times it by itself)
    e) n²

Q5 a) 2
    b) 4
    c) 8
    d) 1024
    (i) multiply 2 by itself n times
    (ii) 2ⁿ

Page 47

Q1 a) 6, 8, 10, 12
    b) 13, 14, 15, 16
    c) 3, 5, 7, 9, 11, 13
    d) 80, 9, 10, 11, 120, 130
    e) 12, 11, 10, 9, 8, 7
    f) 1, 1.5, 2, 2.5, 3, 3.5

Q2 a) x → x + 1
    b) x → 3x
    c) x → 2x
    d) x → 2x + 1

Q3 a) x − 1
    b) 1/3 x
    c) 1/2 x or 0.5 x
    d) 1/2 (x − 1)

Page 48

Q1

x	-3	-2	-1	0	1	2	3
y	-3	-2	-1	0	1	2	3

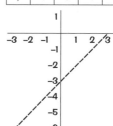

Q2

x	-3	-2	-1	0	1	2	3
y	-1	0	1	2	3	4	5

Q3

x	-3	-2	-1	0	1	2	3
y	-6	-5	-4	-3	-2	-1	0

Q4 All straight lines, all parallel, intercepts
    at (0,0), (0,2), (0,-3)

The Answers

Q5

x	-3	-2	-1	0	1	2	3
y	-6	-4	-2	0	2	4	6

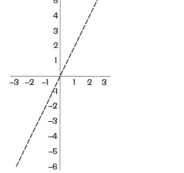

Q6

x	-3	-2	-1	0	1	2	3
y	-9	-6	-3	0	3	6	9

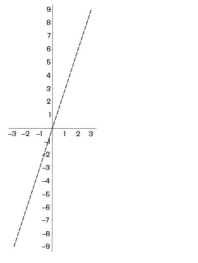

Q7 All straight lines, all pass through (0,0), different steepness/gradient

Page 49

Q1 a) £23
b&c)

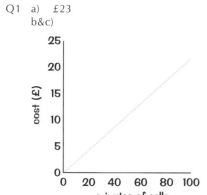

d) £4.60
e) £20.70
f) 25 min
g) approx 65 min

Q2 a)

no. of minutes	0	10	20	30	50	100
cost (£)	10	10.50	11	11.50	12.50	15

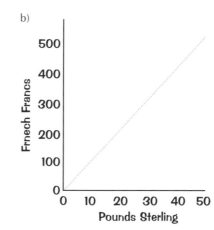

d) £12.00
e) 80 minutes
g) Geri's is better if you make loads of calls.
h) Ali's (£4.60, Geri's £11.00)
i) Geri's (£14.50, Ali's £20.70)

Page 50

Q1 a) £10 gives 105 Francs
£20 gives 210 Francs
£50 gives 525 Francs

b)

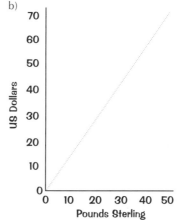

c) 367.5 (though 5 either side is fine)
d) About £24

Q2 a) £10 gives 14 US dollars
£20 gives 28 US dollars
£50 gives 70 US dollars
b)

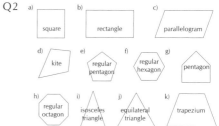

c) 49 (or 3 on either side)
d) £178.57. 250 ÷ 1.4 = £178.57

Q3

b) Intermediate points not valid, in March temp falls sharply at night

Q4 a) 6
b) 3
c) 2
d) 4 or 5
e) 4 or 5
f) 1

Page 51

Q1 a) parallel
b) perpendicular
c) DC
d) EB
e) isosceles triangle
f) right-angled triangle
g) parallelogram
h) trapezium
i) 70
j) 70
k) 70
l) BC = FD
m) FB = BD = DC

Q2 a) square b) rectangle c) parallelogram
d) kite e) regular pentagon f) regular hexagon g) pentagon
h) regular octagon i) isosceles triangle j) equilateral triangle k) trapezium

Page 52

Q1 a) a = 30°, b = 150°
b) c = 30°, d = 30°
c) e = 134°
d) f = 331°
e) g = 61°
f) h = 50°
g) i = 72°
h) j = 45°

Q2 a) a = 50°
b) b = 30°
c) c = 20°
d) d = 57°
e) e = 77°
f) f = 66°

The Answers

Page 53

Q1

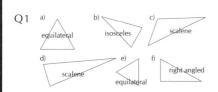

a) equilateral b) isosceles c) scalene d) scalene e) equilateral f) right-angled

Q2

a) irregular and concave b) kite c) parallelogram d) square e) trapezium f) irregular and convex g) rhombus h) rectangle

Q3

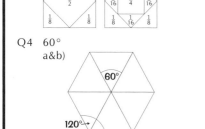

Q4 60°

a&b)

c) The interior angles in a regular hexagon are twice as big as in an equilateral triangle, (ie 60° in the triangle, so 120° in the hexagon).

Page 54

Q1 a)

size of square	1 × 1	2 × 2	3 × 3	4 × 4
number of 1 × 1 squares	1	4	9	16
number of 2 × 2 squares	0	1	4	9
number of 3 × 3 squares	0	0	1	4
number of 4 × 4 squares	0	0	0	1
total number of squares	1	5	14	30

b) Each row is a list of square numbers, 1, 4, 9... Therefore the total number of squares is the sum of all the squares of numbers equal to and below the size of the square. eg 3 × 3 total = $1^2 + 2^2 + 3^2$ = 14.

c) 5 × 5: $1^2 + 2^2 + 3^2 + 4^2 + 5^2$ = 55.

d) 5 × 5 square to confirm answer in c.

Q2 There are a number of possibilities but examples are given below:

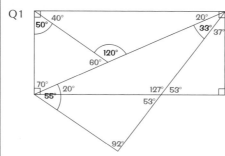

Q3
$$A\hat{E}F = E\hat{B}C = A\hat{C}B = E\hat{C}D = 40°$$
$$A\hat{B}E = A\hat{C}E = C\hat{E}B = B\hat{A}C = C\hat{D}E = 50°$$
$$A\hat{F}E = B\hat{F}C = 100°$$
$$B\hat{F}A = C\hat{F}E = 80°$$

a) Any three, eg: ABCE, BEDC, CDEF

b) all angles in each quadrilateral add up to 360°.

Page 55

Q1

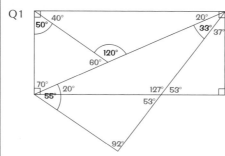

Q2 a) A = 72°, B = 252°.
b) C = 60°, D = 240°.
c) E = 45°, F = 225°.
d) G = 36°, H = 216°.

Q3

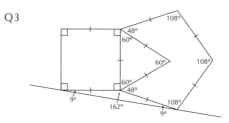

Q4 a) Rhombus (or square possibly)
b) Derrrrrrr... You've got to cut it.

Page 56

Q1 a number of possibilities, egs shown below:

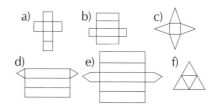

Q2

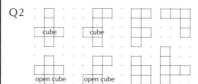

cube cube open cube open cube

Q3

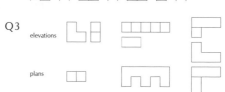

elevations

plans

Q4

Page 57

Q1

Q2

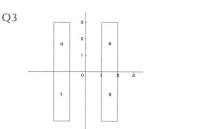

Q3

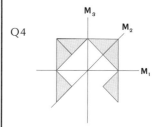

d) reflection in y axis

Q4

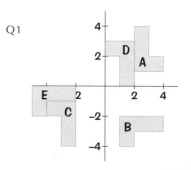

1 line of symmetry (M₃)

Page 58

Q1

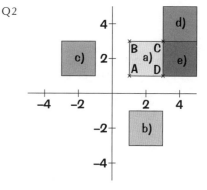

Q2

The Answers

Q3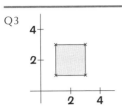

a)   A(1,3), B(3,3), C(3,1), D (1,1)
b)   A(3,3), B(3,1), C(1,1), D (1,3)
c)   A(3,1), B(1,1), C(1,3), D (3,3)
d)   All rotations within original square

Q4   Any suitable diagrams.

Page 59

Q1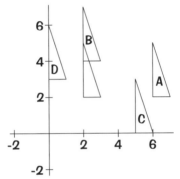

e)   2 units right, 1 unit down (2,-1)
f)   1 unit right, 2 units up (1,2)

Q2   a)   right 4, up 2 (4,2)
b)   right 3, down 6 (3,-6)
c)   left 3, down 7 (-3,-7)
d)   left 8, down 6 (-3,-6)
e)   left 7 (-7,0)
f)   left 11 (-11,0)
g)   right 11 (11,0)
h)   left 10, up 6 (-10,6)

Q3   a)   translation right 6, up 3 (6, 3)
b)   reflection line y = 4.5
c)   rotation 180° centre (0,0) or
     reflection in x axis and y axis
d)   reflection in x axis
e)   translation right 12, up 8 (12, 8)
f)   reflection in line y = -4, and
     reflection in x= -6. OR rotation
     180° about (-6,-4)
g)   rotation anticlockwise 90° centre
     (0,0)
h)   reflection in line x = 5
i)   reflection in y axis
j)   reflection in y axis

Page 60

Q1   FISH

Q2   a)   (4,4)
b)   (1,1)
c)   (5,0)
d)   (-3,-3)
e)   (10,7)
f)   (4,6)
g)   (0,8)
h)   3 possible (8,0) or (-4,0) or (4,-8)

Q3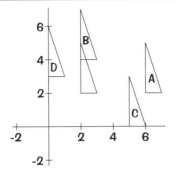

The new coordinates are:
1   (1,0)
2   (1,1)
3   (-1,1)
4   (-1,-1)
5   (2,-1)
6   (2,2)
7   The pattern will be a spiral.

Page 61

Q1   All to within +/- 1 mm:
a)   40 mm
b)   33 mm
c)   52 mm
d)   66 mm
e)   60 mm
f)   47 mm
g)   6 mm
h)   15 mm

Q2   All to within 2 degrees:
a)   230°
b)   24°
c)   113°
d)   337°
e)   173°
f)   86°
g)   54°
h)   98°

Q3   a) i)   ii)
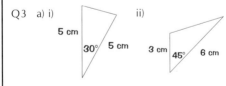

iii)   iv)
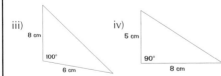

b) i)   ii)
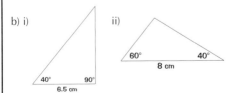

c) i)   ii)

Q4 a)   b)
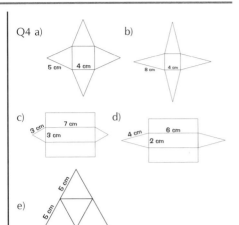

Page 62

Q1   a)   300 cm = 3000 mm
b)   250 cm = 2500 mm
c)   5 m = 5000 mm
d)   1 m = 100 cm
e)   5.5 m = 550 cm
f)   50 cm = 500 mm
g)   5700 m
h)   4.4 km

Q2   a)   100 cl = 1000 ml
b)   200 cl = 2000 ml
c)   3.5 l = 3500 ml
d)   0.5 l = 50 cl
e)   2 kg
f)   7400 g
g)   1 000 000 g = 1000 kg
h)   9.3 tonnes

Q3   a)   10 000 cm²
b)   15 000 cm²
c)   100 mm²
d)   3 cm²
e)   100 000 cm²
f)   10 000 cm² = 1 000 000 mm²

Q4   a)   1.7 kg
b)   1.3 kg
c)   4.1 g
d)   8.6 g
e)   21.5 °C
f)   6.0 °C
g)   83.5°
h)   31.0°
i)   1 hour 14 minutes 52.7 seconds
j)   47 minutes 26.1 seconds

Q5   Lucy's list: 41 km = 25.6 miles,
     3.4 kg = 7.6 lb,
     0.75 litres = 1.2 pints,
     125 g = 0.27 lb = 4.4 oz,
     1.9 m = 2.1 yd = 76 inches
     Grandad's list: 224 miles = 358.4 km,
     6 gallons = 30 litres,
     82 inches = 205 cm = 2.05 m,
     6 lb = 2.7 kg = 2700g

The Answers

Page 63

Q1 a) Acute
    b) Acute
    c) Obtuse
    d) Right-angle
    e) Reflex
    f) Acute
    g) Obtuse

Q2 All to within 5 degrees:
    a) 10°
    b) 30°
    c) 90°
    d) 120°
    e) 45°
    f) 270°
    g) 60°
    h) 315°

Q3 a) 90°
    b) 180°
    c) 270°
    d) 270°
    e) 135°
    f) 45°

Q4 a) 90°
    b) 270°
    c) 90°
    d) 180°
    e) 45°
    f) 135°

Q5 a) drink
    b) book
    c) dog
    d) drink
    e) doll
    f) sweets

Page 64

Q1 a) perimeter 14 cm, area 10 cm², tri 5cm²
    b) 12 m, 8 m², 4 m²
    c) 20 cm, 21 cm², 10.5 cm²
    d) 36 m, 72 m², 36 m²
    e) 2.2 m, 0.1 m², 0.05 m²
        OR 220 cm, 1000 cm², 500 cm²
    f) 8 cm, 3 cm², 1.5 cm²

Q2 a) area 36 m²   perim 28 m
    b) area 9 m²   perim 20 m
    c) area 42 cm² perim 38 cm
    d) area 87 mm² perim 56 mm
    e) area 75 cm² perim 46 cm

Q3 a) 24 cm²
    b) 8 cm
    c) 2 cm
    d) 6 cm
    e) 2 cm

Q4

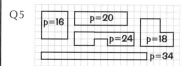

These are just examples, not the definite answer. Different shapes would be acceptable.

Q5

These are just examples, not the definite answer. Different shapes would be acceptable.

Q6 a) 2 m by 9 m
    b) 5 cm by 6 cm
    c) 7 cm by 7 cm → 49 cm²
    d) height 4 m

Page 65

Q1 a) 24
    b) 6
    c) 2 at 6 cm², 2 at 12 cm², 2 at 8 cm²
    d) 52 cm²

Q2 1a) 3 cm³   b) 14 cm²
    2a) 125 mm³   b) 150 mm²
    3a) 500 m³   b) 400 m²

Q3 a) 6 cm³
    b) 13.5 cm³
    c) 5 cm³

Q4 a) 12 by 1 by 1, 2 by 2 by 3, 1 by 2 by 6, 1 by 3 by 4
    b) 2 by 2 by 3
    c) 1 by 1 by 24, 1 by 2 by 12, 1 by 3 by 8, 1 by 4 by 6, 2 by 2 by 6, 2 by 3 by 4
    d) 2 by 3 by 4

Page 66

Q1 a) e.g. count cars/lorries/vans/number of children/number of parked cars/ safe places to cross/speed of cars etc.
    b) Start and end of school. That's when the traffic problems will happen because of everyone going to or from the school.
    c) She's likely to finish work a couple of hours after the school kids go home.

Q2 a) e.g rural/urban, length of journey, traffic safety, parents rushing to get to work.
    b) pupil's own answers

Q3 a) e.g. number of pictures, size of type, length of book/words/ sentences
    b) Depends on answers to 'a)'.

Q4 a) Sensible answers.
    b) Sensible answers.
    c) Sensible answers — show mathematical process behind reasoning.

Page 67

Q1 a) mixed ages, different days, different sexes etc. Repeated and frequent random selection.
    b) yes, by repeating the survey several times with a good cross-section of pupils.

Q2 a) what and when they eat, how much and how often they eat.
    b) no; a representative sample is good enough.
    c) no; too small a sample — the people she surveys might not represent the average customer.

Q3 a) only people not at work/school etc. only good for daytime programmes.
    b) only children
    c) quite good, but maybe few people with day jobs — would be good for daytime TV.
    d) only wealthy people
    e) quite good but no children
    f) only London, maybe lots of people from same ethnic group
    g) The sample size is too small
    Choose e and b together to get both adults and children.

Q4 Census returns or registers of births

Page 68

Q1 Something similar to this:

Vehicle type	Tally			
	10:00-10:15	10:15-10:30	10:30-10:45	10:45-11:00
car				
van				
lorry				
bicycle				
motorcycle				
tractor				
other				

The Answers

Q2 a) Something similar to this:
How do you travel to school?

☐ By car
☐ By bus
☐ On foot
☐ By bicycle
☐ other ....

b) Something similar to this:
How long does it take you to get to school?

☐ 0 – 15 minutes
☐ 16 – 30 minutes
☐ 31 – 45 minutes
☐ 46 – 60 minutes
☐ above 60 minutes

c) Something similar to this:
Do you travel on your own? YES/NO

d) Something similar to this:
Is public transport available? YES/NO
Do you use public transport? YES/NO

Q3 Something similar to this

Sentence Length	Tally
1-5 words	
6-10 words	
11-15 words	
16-20 words	
21-25 words	
26 and over	

Q4 a) 0 - 30 minutes
31 minutes to 1 hour
1 hour to 2 hours
3 hour to 4 hours
more than 4 hours

b) Something similar to this:
1) Are you going to work?
2) How long does the journey normally take?

Sentence Length	Tally
0-30 minutes	
30 minutes to 1 hour	
1 to 2 hours	
2 to 3 hours	
3 to 4 hours	
over 4 hours	

Q5 Things like:
1. Only caters for people who live exactly 1, 2, 3, 4, and 5 miles away. It should be in bands e.g. 0 to 1 mile. Needs higher final band, like "5+ miles".
2. The question is too open.
3. There needs to be a higher option, like 31+ people or something.
4. There needs to be a higher band e.g. above 5 hours.
Needs to say "How much television do you watch per day?" (or week).

Page 69

Q1 a) 8
b) 21
c) 0.4
d) 7 and 10
e) 106

Q2 a) median 6, range 5
b) 6, 10
c) 0.34, 0.6
d) 14, 10
e) 94, 7
f) 38.5, 13

Q3 a) 6
b) 27
c) 105
d) 1.77 to 2 d.p.

Q4 a) median 14 mode 14
b) $5\frac{1}{2}$, $5\frac{1}{2}$
c) 6 mths, 6 mths
d) 100 g, 150 g

Page 70

Q1 a) 212 kg
b) 144 kg
c) 356 kg
d) 50.9 kg

Q2 53.1 kg = $((3\times56)+(4\times51))\div7$

Q3 5, 5, 9, 10, 11

Q4 11, 13, 15, 15, 16

Q5 29

Q6 a) mean 15.35 median 15½
mode 15½ range 2½

b) mean 20.3 median 23
mode   23   range 29

c) mean £5.68   median £4.90
mode £5.60 & £6.10   range £12.30

d) mean 8.5   median 9
mode 1   range 16

e) mean £16 450   median £10 250 mode £5600 range £50 400

f) mean £2514 median £10
mode £10 range £24990

g) mean 19.3   median 19.5
mode 2, 36 & 37   range 36

Page 71

Q1

Favourite TV Soap	Number of Viewers	Degrees
Riverside	15	30°
Westenders	45	90°
Far and Away	30	60°
Grimdale	30	60°
Abdication Street	60	120°
TOTAL	180	360°

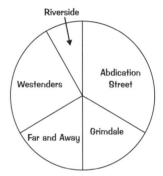

Q2

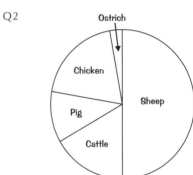

Q3

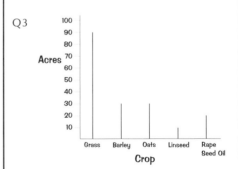

Q4

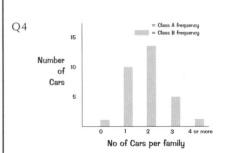

Class B tend to have more cars per family than Class A. The average in B appears to be higher than in A.

The Answers

Page 72

Q1 a) Diane: 150°, Sally: 90°, Emma: 45°, Liz: 60°, Kate: 15°
b) 1/4
c) 720
d) 300
e) Kate

Q2 a) Jimmy has eaten 5 times as many pies as James. James' cheese and onion area is not 5 times bigger than Jimmy's cheese and onion area, so he's eaten fewer pies. (OR... 500 ÷ 360 = 1.39 pies per degree. Jimmy's cheese and onion area is 56° so 56 × 1.39 = 78 cheese and onion pies. 100 ÷ 360 = 0.28 pies per degree. James' cheese and onion area is 198° so 198 × 0.28 = 55 cheese and onion pies.)
b) 125. Looks like a quarter of the pie chart (and it is — though it's best to check the angle's 90° using a set square or protractor), so that's a quarter of the pies, which is 125 (500 ÷ 4 = 125).

Q3 a) 3/5
b) 1/50
c) 36°
d) education: £180 million, social services: £60 million, roads and transport: £30 million, waste management: £18 million fire and rescue: £6 million, libraries and recreation: £6 million.

Q4 a) 30
b) Tennis
c) 15

Page 73

Q1 a) Book B
b) No, need to know what it is about

Q2 a) School A
b) School B
c) 10

Q3 a) Appleton
b) Orangeburgh

Q4 a) Monday, Wednesday and Friday
b) Thursday
c) Bodgit

Page 74

Q1 a) impossible
b) certain
c) likely/unlikely
d) unlikely (or maybe likely)
e) impossible
f) likely/unlikely
g) impossible
h) likely/unlikely

Q2 a) unlikely
b) more likely
c) more likely
d) less likely

Q3 Pupil's own answers

Q4 a) Higher. Either: "two is one of the lowest numbers from one to ten" or a better answer: "Out of the remaining cards, only one of them is lower than two, so it's not likely she'll draw that."
b) Impossible. Because the 2 and the 1 have been drawn, the lowest card is a 3, which is higher than 1.

Page 75

Q1

```
0                              1
a   d e         c        f    b
```

Q2 a) 1/2
b) 1/2
c) 2/3
d) 1/2
e) 1/3
f) 0

Q3 a) 1/13
b) 2/13
c) 0
d) 5/13

Q4 a) 1/2
b) 1/10
c) 1/10
d) 1/5
e) 0
f) 3/10

Page 76

Q1 a) Cannot be certain
b) Cannot be certain
c) Probably not because after 100 tosses the head and tail count is pretty even.
d) Probably because the probability of getting 31 or fewer heads on an even coin after 100 throws is very low.

Q2 pupil's own answers

Page 77

Q1 a) 5
b) 50
c) 250
d) 1
e) 10
f) 50

Q2 a) 1/5
b) 2

c) 20
d) 100

Q3 a) 0.2
b) 160
c) 160

Q4 a) The frequencies should add up to 10. The distribution might not be even.
b) They should be spread out pretty well, though slight clustering is fine.
c) 20 numbers — more even spread. 50 numbers — close to even spread of numbers.